Before his retirement fro
Dr. Carl Armerding was p... Bible and Theology at Wheaton College (Ill.). He has served on the faculty and in the extension department of Moody Bible Institute. He was professor of Homiletics at Dallas Theological Seminary for about five years.

He received an honorary doctorate from Dallas Theological Seminary and graduated from the University of New Mexico with a B.A. degree.

Dr. Armerding is president emeritus of Central American Missions headquartered in Dallas. He is very much in demand as a conference speaker.

Among his many works, he has authored *Signs of Christ's Coming* (a study of Matthew 24 and the return of Christ that will reverse the world situation), *Conquest and Victory,* and *Esther.*

PSALMS IN A
MINOR KEY

PSALMS IN A
MINOR KEY

By

CARL ARMERDING

To
the children whom God has given me
Miriam and Hudson
Louise and Bob
Winnie and Jack
Jeanie and Dan

MOODY PRESS

CHICAGO

Printed in the United States of America

CONTENTS

PREFACE

IN SELECTING the psalms included in this book, much thought was given to the various life situations presented in each of them. The book of the Psalms is largely a book of experience. And many of them deal with experiences which are strikingly similar to our own. It is this that makes them both relevant and meaningful for us. Others might have been included, such as the twenty-second and the sixty-ninth. But these belong in a more specialized category, such as the Messianic psalm. Other psalms were omitted to avoid repetition. Then, too, it was thought best not to attempt anything exhaustive, but rather to make these studies suggestive, so that the reader may discover similar treasures for himself in other parts of this incomparable collection of inspired poems.

Free use was made of illustrations, many of them from the author's own experience, which it is hoped will make these meditations of practical use for those who have the responsibility of ministering to others. In other words, these studies are intended to be contemporary.

The title of this book was suggested by a statement made by the apostle Paul who said, "We know that the whole creation groaneth and travaileth in pain together until now. And not only they, but ourselves also, which have the firstfruits of the Spirit, even we ourselves groan within ourselves, waiting for the adoption, to wit, the redemption of our body" (Ro 8:22-23). But "groanings which can not be uttered" will one day give place to songs of joy. In keeping with this, many psalms which begin in a minor key conclude with notes of praise and worship.

1

PSALM 3

Outnumbered, But Not Overcome

THE THIRD PSALM is the first in a series of psalms, all of which seem to have grown out of some bitter experience. With the exception of the fourth psalm, they all refer to enemies of one kind or another. But the closing verses of all except the sixth are full of blessing, praise, and peace. Even the sixth psalm is not without its bright spots, because in it there is the assurance that the Lord has heard, and that He will receive the prayer of the afflicted one.

Many believe that these psalms will yet be used by the godly remnant of Israel during the great tribulation. But that need not hinder us from making a present use of them. Every Scripture is divinely inspired and profitable for teaching, conviction, correction, and instruction in righteousness: that the man of God may be complete, fully competent for every good work. They have a contemporary value, no matter what their final import may be.

Ever since the fall of Adam, this world has felt the effects of his disobedience. The true child of God has never been without strong opposition from the forces of evil. Ever since the day that Cain killed his brother, the world, the flesh, and the devil have hated the man of faith. Therefore we need not think it "strange concerning the fiery trial which is to try [us], as though some strange thing happened unto [us]" (1 Pe 4:12). Nevertheless, it is important that we should know how to act when the enemy attacks; to know what resources we have, and how to make the best possible use of them.

Our enemy seldom works single-handedly. He has many allies, and he loves to impress us with the number of those that are on his side. Evidently he used this method with the psalmist.

9

Hence the prayer: "LORD, how are they increased that trouble me!
many are they that rise up against me" (Ps 3:1). Apparently
there is no limit to the number of recruits available. And he loves
to parade them before us in order to fill our hearts with fear and
despair.

A good illustration of this is found in 2 Kings 6:15-17. The
king of Syria had surrounded Elisha by night, with a great host
of horses and chariots, intending to capture him in the morning.
"And when the servant of the man of God was risen early, and
gone forth, behold, an host compassed the city both with horses
and chariots. And his servant said unto him, Alas, my master!
how shall we do? And he answered, Fear not; for they that be
with us are more than they that be with them. And Elisha prayed,
and said, LORD, I pray thee, open his eyes that he may see. And
the LORD opened the eyes of the young man; and he saw: and,
behold, the mountain was full of horses and chariots of fire around
about Elisha." And we are just as well protected now, because
God's angels are "all ministering spirits, sent forth to minister
for them who shall be heirs of salvation" (Heb 1:14).

Not only does our enemy seek to impress us with numbers, he
also tries to discourage us by what they say. "Many there be
which say of my soul, There is no help for him in God" (Ps 3:2).
And there are no words that wound more deeply than those that
suggest that God has forsaken us. The enemy knows that if he
can make us doubt God's loving care for us, he will have scored
a victory over us. Even though we know from experience that
the Lord does care for us, we often raise the question, "Carest
Thou not that we perish?"

Such a question is very often the echo of something the enemy
has said. He may not have said it to us directly. He simply got
someone to say in our hearing, "His God is no help to him now."
Had he come to us directly and said, "There is no help for you in
God," we probably would have withstood him to his face. He
uses the indirect method because it suits his purpose better. He
knows as well as you and I that there *is* help for us "in God." But
he would discourage us from availing ourselves of that help.

He may even use the argument that we do not deserve help.
And we all have to admit that that is true. We do not deserve
anything. But our God does not deal with us according to our

deserts. He is the God of all grace. His throne is a throne of grace. And He gives more grace.

Therefore we must take our eyes off the enemy and his hosts and fix them on the Lord. This is exactly what the psalmist did when he said, "But, thou, O LORD, art a shield for me," or, "about me." What a wonderful difference it makes when we put Him between us and the foe. Immediately we discover that we have perfect protection not merely on one side but all around us. Long before the psalmist's day, the Lord had said to Abram, "Fear not, Abram: I am thy shield, and thy exceeding great reward" (Gen 15:1).

I believe that this is the key to what Paul meant when he wrote, "Above all, taking the shield of faith" (Eph 6:16). For years I understood those words to mean that "above all" of the armor mentioned in that chapter, I should take my faith as a shield. But when I tried that, I found that my faith was more like a sieve than a shield. So I looked at the text again to see if I had by any chance misread it. No, there it was: "the shield of faith." But then it occurred to me that it might have been rendered "faith's shield" without changing the meaning of the original. And it made a world of difference when I read it that way! Now it was no longer my feeble faith that was to be my shield, but rather the shield which faith takes—the Lord Himself. He is an integral part of the whole armor of God. And to have the Lord as my shield means a great deal more than the strongest faith I ever had.

The battle with Satan and his hosts is no light skirmish. The best of saints have trembled as they have wrestled, not against flesh and blood, but against principalities, powers, the rulers of the darkness of this world, and against wicked agents in high places (Eph 6:12). Nothing short of divine protection can avail in the fight against such supernatural enemies. But when the battle is over and the victory won, we can rejoice, because the Lord is not only our shield but also our glory and the "lifter up" of our heads. The child of God has something more dependable than the most stable government this world has ever known. Thrones topple, rulers flee, governments are overthrown. Yes, even heaven and earth shall pass away. But our Lord is the same yesterday, today, and forever. No change Jehovah knows. And He is "my glory, and the lifter up of mine head" (Ps 3:3).

Thus encouraged, the psalmist now turns to others with a word of testimony. First of all (v. 4), he speaks as one who knows from experience that God is a prayer-hearing and a prayer-answering God. "I cried . . . and he heard." One need not be a Christian very long before he is able to say that. The promises of God are something more than pretty sayings with which to adorn our bedroom walls. They have stood, and will stand, the hardest usage. And happy is the man who has a good list of answered prayers which he may use to strengthen the faith of some faltering brother in Christ, or, on the other hand to silence some unbeliever. The record of answered prayers is one of the best of apologetics. It is no wonder that it was the first thing the psalmist used in his testimony to others.

When I was a young man, I knew a Christian doctor who used such a record with good effect. In an ordinary loose-leaf book, he wrote down things that he had prayed for, and the dates when he first prayed for them, one request to a page. Under each request he recorded the dates when he repeated the request. In not a few cases the prayer was answered the same day, or soon after. But there were also times when a particular request was repeated many times. At the bottom of the page, he recorded the date the prayer was answered. On some pages, however, the space was blank, indicating that the answer had either been deferred or denied. But the favorable answers far outnumbered the deferments or denials. When I inquired what use he made of that book, he told me that he had used it many times to encourage the feeble faith of some of his Christian patients. But he also used it in witnessing to his non-Christian patients, hoping that they too might come to know the Lord "who only doeth wondrous things" (Ps 72:18).

At times, the Lord hears our prayers but does not grant our requests. Recall that the apostle Paul besought the Lord three times to remove the thorn in the flesh, "the messenger of Satan," sent to buffet him, lest he should be exalted above measure. The answer was, "My grace is sufficient for thee: for my strength is made perfect in weakness" (2 Co 12:7-9). Evidently he was perfectly satisfied with the answer because he goes on to say, "Most gladly therefore will I rather glory in my infirmities, that the power of Christ may rest upon me." As the psalmist says here, "The

LORD sustained me." He not only gives sustaining grace, He himself sustains.

Such grace begets courage. Therefore "I will not be afraid of ten thousands of people, that have set themselves against me round about" (Ps 3:6). This is something more than fleshly bravado. It is the courage of one who has entered into the full enjoyment of what it means to have the Lord Himself as a shield about him. With such a shield, it matters not how many may threaten him; he is fully protected.

But we must distinguish between courage and self-confidence. There is a difference. While on the one hand he says, "I will not be afraid," on the other he prays, "Arise, O LORD; save me, O my God" (v. 7). Such a prayer is not one of fear or unbelief; it expresses complete dependence upon the Lord. No matter how many victories he may have won, he is still the dependent one who has no confidence in himself. Like the apostle Paul, he could "boast in Christ Jesus, and have no confidence in the flesh." Certainly, it was not a case of fresh fear taking hold of him. The language which follows proves that. He says, "Thou hast smitten all mine enemies upon the cheek bone; thou hast broken the teeth of the ungodly." A man who is afraid does not talk like that. Even though he prays for help, he sees his foes already smitten and disabled.

I recall an experience I had some years ago while visiting a zoo. I paused before the cage of a wildcat, wondering just what purpose wildcats might serve in God's great creation. While I stood there, an attendant entered the cage with nothing in his hands but a broom. After carefully closing the door through which he had just entered, he began to sweep the cage's floor. He seemed not to have the slightest fear of the wildcat, which lay as if asleep in a corner of the cage. To my surprise, the beast made no move until the attendant gave him a shove with the broom. Then it merely backed away and lay down again. At that point I said to the attendant, "You certainly are a brave man to go in there with nothing in your hands but a broom."

"Nah," he replied, "I'm not brave."

"Well, then," said I, "that wildcat must be tame."

"Nah," he answered, "he isn't tame."

"Well," said I again, "if you are not brave and he is not tame, how do you account for the fact that he does not attack you?"

He replied simply, "He's old. He hasn't got any teeth."

As I continued my walk, I pondered these words, *no teeth*. And I remembered the Scripture which says, "Be sober, be vigilant; because your adversary the devil, as a roaring lion, walketh about, seeking whom he may devour: Whom resist stedfast in the faith" (1 Pe 5:8-9*a*). But, like the psalmist, we may consider him as one whose teeth are already broken. We are told to resist him and he will flee from us (Ja 4:7). "In all these things we are more than conquerors through him that loved us" (Ro 8:37).

Then we too may end our psalm on a positive note. "Salvation [deliverance] belongeth unto the LORD: thy blessing is upon thy people. Selah."

When Jonah celebrated in this way, the Lord commanded the fish and it delivered up Jonah, safe and sound, upon the dry land. But it is to be noted that he celebrated before the deliverance actually took place. No doubt such was the case with the psalmist also. Faith does things like that. It "calleth those things which be not as though they were" (Ro 4:17).

Through faith the psalmist emerged from fear and doubt to triumph and victory even though, to begin with, he was outnumbered. But he was not overcome. "Thanks be to God, which giveth us the victory through our Lord Jesus Christ" (1 Co 15:57).

> Ye fearful saints, fresh courage take,
> The clouds ye so much dread
> Are big with mercy, and shall break
> In blessings on your head.
>
> WILLIAM COWPER

2

PSALM 4

An Interrupted Prayer

THIS PSALM divides quite naturally into three parts, the first and last of which constitute a prayer, and a middle section which is an interruption. We know from experience how easily our prayers are interrupted. Sometimes this occurs without our knowing just how, especially when one is praying silently and the mind unconsciously wanders off to other things. That certainly is not the case here, even if we leave out of account for the time being that this psalm, like all of Scripture, is divinely inspired. The interruption here is deliberate. It appears that the psalmist began with prayer, then he preached, after which he resumed his prayer.

I know of no other prayer recorded in Scripture that begins like this one. The Lord Jesus addressed the Father as "righteous Father" (Jn 17:25). But to address God as "the God of my righteousness" is different. It implies that one has given up his own righteousnesses which, after all, are only "filthy rags" (Is 64:6), for "the righteousness which is of God by faith" (Phil 3:9). Because of this, one may confidently draw near to the throne of grace and cry, "Hear me when I call, O God of my righteousness."

The second part of this prayer has to do with a fruitful experience. "Thou has enlarged me when I was in distress," or, as another translation has it, "In pressure Thou has enlarged me." We hear a great deal about pressure and tension these days. Where there is pressure, there is bound to be tension. And, come to think of it, we could not get along very well without them. Without pressure, an automobile would be useless. The pressure in the engine supplies the power. And the pressure in the tires makes for comfort. The tension in a musical instrument such as the violin

15

or piano enables the musician to produce the music which delights our ears. When we transfer these things to ourselves, we consider them calamities instead of assets.

Of course, it is true that pressure may be increased beyond reasonable limits. And then an explosion occurs. The tension on a string may be increased to the point where the string snaps. But God is faithful who will not permit us to be tried beyond our endurance, but will with the trial make a way to escape, that we may be able to bear it (1 Co 10:13).

The apostle Paul, referring to an experience he had for Christ's sake, wrote, "We would not, brethren, have you ignorant of our trouble which came to us in Asia, that we were pressed out of measure, above strength, insomuch that we despaired even of life" (2 Co 1:8). But just such experiences made him the great soul that he was.

It may be that some of us have aspired to be great. We may even have prayed to be greatly used of God. Let us not be surprised then if He uses pressure and tension to answer that prayer. Let us be grateful for enlarged spiritual capacity, however painful the process may be. One thing we may always be sure of is sufficient grace, for "He giveth more grace" (Ja 4:6). It was pressure, divinely applied, that made David great. Because of this, we may pray like the psalmist, "Be gracious unto me, and hear my prayer."

It is quite likely that the pressure to which he refers was due to his environment. Evidently the "sons of men" among whom he lived were like those of our times. It grieved him to see them turn his glory into shame. Since he has already told us who his glory is (Ps 3:3), we need not be in doubt about what he means when he says "my glory." He is not talking about any personal glory that might be his but rather about the only one in whom he could glory, the Lord Himself.

How long will ye turn my glory into shame?" (Ps 4:2) is an arresting question. The complete answer to it is found in the first chapter of Romans. There we read of those who knew God, but when they knew Him they glorified Him not as God, neither were they thankful. They became vain in their imaginations, and their foolish heart was darkened. "Professing themselves to be wise, they became fools, And changed the glory of the uncorruptible God into an image made like to corruptible man, and to birds, and four-footed beasts, and creeping things" (Ro 1:22-23). Those who had been made in the image and likeness of God sank to the level of beasts. "Man that is in honour, and understandeth not, is like the beasts that perish" (Ps 49:20).

It is to such that the psalmist addresses himself. He does not ask them why they do this, but, "How long?" He merely deals with the facts in the case without inquiring into causes such as are revealed to us in Romans 1. Do they think that these things will go on indefinitely? Is there no limit to God's patience? And how long will they love vanity, or emptiness? How long will they spend their money for that which is not bread and their "labour for that which satisfieth not"? (Is 55:2).

How well the question fits the day in which we live! If men had to be satisfied with vanity unwillingly, we might well pity them. But the psalmist's question implies that they love it. They prefer it to Him who alone can satisfy. Many of them would resent being offered something better. They would look upon such offers as an invasion of their privacy. They love darkness rather than light because their deeds are evil (Jn 3:19). Man is not the unfortunate individual some would make him out to be. He is no ignoramus; he is a rebel. Refusing the truth, he accepts a lie. "And for this cause God shall send them strong delusion, that they should believe a [the] lie: That they all might be damned who believed not the truth but had pleasure in unrighteousness" (2 Th 2:11-12).

That this sounds harsh I will admit. But if it serves to awaken some soul to his need of Christ, then we may well thank God that He has caused such things to be written. He has no pleasure in the death of the wicked. He is longsuffering and not willing that any should perish. But unbelieving men abuse His patience and neglect so great salvation till "the harvest is past, the summer ended," and they are not saved (Jer 8:20). No doubt the pause ("Selah") at the close of Psalm 4:2 is intended to make men stop and think!

But this is only the introduction to this brief sermon. To ask questions is not enough. Accordingly, the psalmist loses no time in presenting the one who can save men from their sin and shame. In place of vanity, or emptiness, He can give fullness of life. In contrast to "the lie" He is "the truth" (Jn 14:6). In presenting this one, the psalmist does not indulge in mere oratorical propriety.

He does not say "Please be advised," and so on; "But know that the LORD hath set apart him that is godly for himself" (Ps 4:3). It seems quite clear to me that he is referring here to "Him, whom the Father hath sanctified, and sent into the world" (Jn 10:36); the truly pious one whom the Father has set apart and sent "into the world, that we might live through him" (1 Jn 4:9). Holy, harmless, and undefiled, "He is able to save them to the uttermost that come unto God by Him" (Heb 7:25). And because of Him each one of us can say, "The LORD will hear when I call unto him" (Ps 4:3).

But there is much more involved in the presentation of "him that is godly" at this point. Undoubtedly this was intended to have its due effect on the "sons of men" to whom he has been speaking. He bids them "stand in awe" in the presence of this godly one. When Job stood in His presence, he said, "I have heard of thee by the hearing of the ear: but now mine eye seeth thee. Wherefore I abhor myself, and repent in dust and ashes" (Job 42:5-6). Likewise Isaiah, when he saw the Lord high and lifted up, said. "Woe is me! for I am undone . . . for mine eyes have seen the King, the LORD of hosts" (Is 6:5). Face to face with "him that is godly" they learned how far short they had come of "the glory of God" (Ro 3:23) shining "in the face of Jesus Christ" (2 Co 4:6). This is the perfect standard by which God measures men.

The psalmist goes on to say, "And sin not," which might have been rendered "do not miss, or forfeit;" suggesting that this is indeed a crucial moment, a time for honest introspection.

"Commune with your own heart upon your bed, and be still" (Ps 4:4). Very appropriately, we find the word *selah* again at this point. Take your time; do not be in a hurry. And then if the question be asked, "What do I do next?" the answer is clear, "Offer the sacrifices of righteousness, and put your trust in the LORD" (v. 5).

The psalmist lived in a time when the animal sacrifices prescribed by the law of Moses were still being offered. "But in those sacrifices there is a remembrance again made of sins every year. For it is not possible that the blood of bulls and of goats should take away sins" (Heb 10:3-4). Nevertheless they prefigured Him who was to offer "one sacrifice for sins" (Heb 10:12). And this He did at Calvary, when He gave Himself an offering and a sacrifice to

God for us (Eph 5:2). In Him are found all the "sacrifices of righteousness." He is the all-sufficient one. More than this I do not need; less than this I dare not bring to God. But I must come in faith. And that is the concluding note in this brief sermon. "Put your trust in the LORD" (Ps 4:5). Or, as the apostle Paul said to the Philippian jailer, "Believe on the Lord Jesus Christ, and thou shalt be saved, and thy house" (Ac 16:31).

Having delivered this brief, but comprehensive message to the sons of men, the psalmist now resumes his prayer. But instead of a glowing account of great blessing as a result, he has to report that many are saying, "Who will shew us any good?" (v. 6). But what do they mean by "good"? For the psalmist there is nothing better than the light of the LORD's countenance. It is the only thing for which he prays specifically in this psalm. He would rather reflect the glory of the Lord than to have all the wealth in the world. Nor is he selfish in this desire. He prays, "LORD, lift thou up the light of thy countenance upon us." In like manner the apostle Paul could write, "But we all, with open [or, unveiled] face beholding as in a glass the glory of the Lord, are changed into the same image from glory to glory, even as by the Spirit of the Lord" (2 Co 3:18).

How few are the radiant countenances these days! One has but to study the faces of men and women as they rush to and fro in an air terminal; or as they check out at a supermarket; or even as they sit in church waiting for the service to begin, should they be among the few who get there that early! Some of these people probably had "morning devotions" before leaving home, but how easy it is to read a portion of Scripture without taking time to behold the glory of the Lord!

Very closely related to a radiant countenance is a glad heart. Note that the psalmist continues his prayer, saying, "Thou hast put gladness in my heart, more than in the time that their corn and their wine increased" (Ps 4:7). He had discovered that a man's life does not consist in the abundance of the things he possesses (Lk 12:15). How few there are who have discovered that in our generation! That is why "joy is withered away from the sons of men" (Joel 1:12). The many attempts to complete the sentence, "Happiness is—" show that no one seems to have a satisfactory answer. And so, in our desperation, we take another tranquilizer.

Evidently the psalmist had no need for such. With calm resolve he says, "I will both lay me down in peace, and sleep: for thou, LORD, only makest me dwell in safety." Such is the perfect peace enjoyed by those whose minds are stayed on Him, because they trust in Him (Is 26:3). No one has ever been able to define it, but there are those who enjoy it, nevertheless. As the Scots would say, "It's better felt than telt."

I was asked on one occasion to define what is meant by the peace "which passeth all understanding" (Phil 4:7). My reply was, "If I could tell you, it would not pass all understanding." And yet, our Saviour's legacy of peace is available to all. "Peace I leave with you, my peace I give unto you: not as the world giveth, give I unto you. Let not your heart be troubled, neither let it be afraid" (Jn 14:27).

Psalm four closes on a threefold chord—light, gladness, and peace. The pressure which was so difficult to bear has given place to a peace that knows no measure; and the prayer that was interrupted, terminates in a serenity that is permanent.

Peace, perfect peace, in this dark world of sin?
The blood of Jesus whispers peace within.

Peace, perfect peace, with sorrows surging round?
On Jesus' bosom naught but calm is found.

Peace, perfect peace, death shadowing us and ours?
Jesus has vanquished death and all its powers.

It is enough: earth's struggles soon shall cease,
And Jesus, call us to heav'n's perfect peace.

E. H. BICKERSTETH

3

PSALM 5

"Lead Me, O Lord, in Thy Righteousness"

THE PROBLEM OF GUIDANCE comes up again and again in the life
of a Christian. With such exceptions as the choice of a life partner,
or of a profession, we find it necessary to seek the Lord's guidance
day after day, and sometimes more than once a day. No doubt
there is design in all of this, because He would have us constantly
looking to Him. A good illustration of this is found in Numbers
9:22. "Whether it were two days, or a month, or a year, that the
cloud tarried upon the tabernacle, remaining thereon, the children
of Israel abode in their tents, and journeyed not." That, of course,
had to do with the nation as a whole. Our more immediate need
is personal guidance. And that is exactly what the psalmist prayed
for. "Lead me, O Lord, in thy righteousness."

David knew where to go for guidance. In verse 7 of Psalm 5,
he says, "But as for me, I will come into thy house in the multitude of thy mercy: and in thy fear will I worship toward thy holy
temple." Evidently it was characteristic of him to go there, because it is the only thing in the life of David to which our Lord
ever made any reference. He said to the Pharisees, "Have ye not
read what David did, when he was an hungered, and they were
with him; How he entered into the house of God" (Mt 12:3-4).
Apparently that was more important than his victory over Goliath,
or any of his military exploits.

The manner of the writer's coming is important. He came as a
suppliant, trusting in the abundance of God's mercy, or loving-
kindness. Then, too, he came in a spirit of worship and reverence,
all of which must be taken into account as we consider the opening words of the psalm. He pleads not only to be heard, but that

21

that which he cannot put into words, the meditation of his heart, may also be considered. We all know what it is to be lost for words, unable to give utterance to the deeper longings of our hearts. There are times when our prayers are but "groanings which cannot be uttered" (Ro 8:26). But whether audible or inaudible, we know that there is one who discerns the thoughts and intents of the heart. It was to Him that the psalmist addressed himself, saying, "Give ear to my words, O LORD, consider my meditation. Hearken unto the voice of my cry, my King, and my God: for unto thee will I pray. My voice shalt thou hear in the morning, O LORD; in the morning will I direct my prayer unto thee, and will look up" (Ps 5:1-3).

The words, the cry, and the voice are audible. The meditation and the look are inaudible. But the look is an upward look and one of expectancy, which often expresses more than spoken words. The deepest kind of prayer is often voiceless. It does not ask for anything; it just pours out its unspoken request in silent communion with God.

But that kind of prayer requires intense concentration. Our minds wander so easily. Therefore we need to "gird up the loins" of our minds, which is just another way of saying, "Concentrate."

The time of day which the psalmist chose for this is also important. "In the morning will I direct my prayer unto thee" (v. 3). If we do not give ourselves to prayer in the morning, we are apt to neglect it altogether. If we allow the morning newspaper or the radio, to claim that prime time, we might as well stay in bed. For the most part, the news is just more of the same anyhow. I had this impressed upon me one morning as I was scanning a newspaper, when a Christian friend of mine entered the room and said, "Well, what's the devil been up to overnight?" And that aptly described what I was reading at the time. If one cannot resist giving such things first place in the morning, it would be better to discontinue getting the morning news altogether.

The great commentator, Delitzsch, has pointed out that the word *direct* is the same as that used to describe the laying of the wood on the altar of sacrifice, and also for the arranging of the parts of the sacrifice. This was the duty of the priest in Israel as the new day began to dawn. Such preparation is no less in order when we draw near to the throne of grace to offer our sacrifices of praise and prayer, and also to renew our devotion as we hail Him again as our King and our God.

At this point, and not before, the psalmist makes known the desire of his heart. "Lead me, O LORD, in thy righteousness because of mine enemies; make thy way straight before my face" (Ps 5:8). This is something more than a request for direction. He wanted to be led by the Lord Himself, who always leads us in "the paths of righteousness for his name's sake" (Ps 23:3). These paths may go through the valley of the shadow of death, but with Him at our side, we have no need to fear.

The psalmist was well aware of the deadly enemies who were watching his every move. That will account for the strong language which we find in some parts of this psalm. These men had rebelled against the Lord; they were liars and bloody men. Such language is not used to describe those who are merely careless or indifferent. In this day of grace, such language does not become us, even though we may feel like praying such a prayer as we behold the open wickedness on every hand. It is then that we have to remember the Lord's words to those who wanted to call down fire from heaven upon their enemies, after the manner of Elijah. "He turned, and rebuked them, and said, Ye know not what manner of spirit ye are of" (Lk 9:55). Nevertheless, the apostle Paul came close to this when he wrote, "Alexander the coppersmith did me much evil: the Lord reward him according to his works: Of whom be thou ware also; for he hath greatly withstood our words" (2 Ti 4:14-15). But in the next verse, he made a difference between Alexander and those who had deserted him in the hour of his need. For them he prayed that it might not be laid to their charge. And that is the proper Christian spirit.

The psalmist closed his prayer on a joyful note. "Let all those that put their trust in thee rejoice: let them ever shout for joy, because thou defendest them: let them also that love thy name be joyful in thee. For, thou, LORD, wilt bless the righteous: with favour wilt thou compass him as with a shield" (Ps 5:11-12). The combination of faith, joy, and love, suggests a chord of music. This psalm was to be sung to the accompaniment of music "upon Nehiloth" (or, flutes), so appropriate to a psalm in a minor key. Plaintive notes may be heard all through this psalm. But even the inarticulate sigh gives way to notes of joy and praise.

Our Saviour said, "Verily, verily, I say unto you, That ye shall weep and lament, but the world shall rejoice: and ye shall be sorrowful, but your sorrow shall be turned into joy" (Jn 16:20).

And the closing words of the psalm give us a fine example of this. All that the psalmist had asked for was guidance. Here he also is assured of blessing and protection. "For, thou, LORD, wilt bless the righteous: with favour wilt thou compass him as with a shield" (v. 12). It just like the Lord to do "exceeding abundantly above all that we ask or think" (Eph 3:20). And that is enough to make our cup run over.

> Lord, 'tis enough, we ask no more:
> Thy grace around us pours
> Its rich and unexhausted store,
> And all its joy is ours.
>
> JOHN NEWTON

4

PSALM 6

"Whom the Lord Loveth He Chasteneth"

THIS PSALM, generally referred to as the first of the seven penitential psalms, presents the psalmist in a situation which is quite common to all true children of God. "For what son is he whom the father chasteneth not?" (Heb 12:7). In chastening us, God deals with us as with sons. But His chastening is not necessarily punitive. As in the case of the apostle Paul, it may be preventive (2 Co 12:7).

In the psalms immediately preceding this, the psalmist complains about his enemies. They were the cause of any grief or sorrow that came to him. In this psalm we note a distinct difference. Here it is the Lord who is dealing with him. Instead of looking around, he is looking within.

Such introspection can be very salutary if kept within bounds. Constant introspection often leads to morbidity. But there are times when it is necessary for one to examine himself, not that he may cease communing, but that he may truly commune with Him whose love is everlasting (cf. 1 Co 11:28). Here, however, the Lord's dealings with him are referred to as His anger and His hot displeasure. Truly, "No chastening for the present seemeth to be joyous, but grievous" (Heb 12:11). But at no time does he charge the Lord with unfairness. Perhaps the real reason for this discipline is not disclosed so that the lessons to be learned may be more generally applied.

In pleading for mercy, the writer of this psalm does not speak as one who is being dealt with unjustly. "Have mercy upon me, O LORD; for I am weak: O LORD, heal me; for my bones are vexed. My soul is also sore vexed" (Ps 6:2-3). In pleading his weakness, he uses a common argument, but he does not use this as an excuse for some fault or sin that he may have committed. He speaks as one who knows that there is a limit to what one can take both physically and emotionally, for his "soul is also sore vexed." Who of us has not felt the same way more than once? It is at such times that we are apt to crack up and even despise the chastening of the Lord.

Eliphaz the Temanite put it well when he said to Job, "Behold, happy is the man whom God correcteth: therefore despise not thou the chastening of the Almighty" (Job 5:17). A similar exhortation occurs in Proverbs 3:11: "My son, despise not the chastening of the LORD; neither be weary of his correction: for whom the LORD loveth he correcteth; even as a father the son in whom he delighteth." To this the writer of Hebrews adds, "And scourgeth every son whom he receiveth." This discipline is a proof both of our sonship and of His love for us. And when He says, "every son," He means that there are no exceptions. And for those who are "exercised thereby" it yields "the peaceable fruit of righteousness" (Heb 12:11). An explanatory comment about this phrase is made by Erich Sauer: "Thus he acquires a 'fruit' which as to the state of his heart is called 'peaceable,' and with respect to his standing and practical state in life is called 'righteousness.' "*

When the psalmist raises the question, How long? he reacts just as any of us would. Some of us have not yet learned to say with Paul, "We glory in tribulations also: knowing that tribulation worketh patience; and patience experience," or, "ripeness of character," as Weymouth put it.

In watching a moth emerge from its cocoon, one may be tempted to help by shortening the process. To have done so, of course, would have resulted in a crippled creature instead of the thing of beauty which finally emerged after a prolonged struggle. Thus nature itself teaches us that there are some things which cannot be hastened. And God's chastening is one of them.

The answer to the question, How long? really rests with ourselves. When we have yielded to the hand that is dealing with us, the healing of body and soul will begin. In that connection it is interesting to observe that in chastening us, the Lord uses but one hand (Ps 32:4), but in healing He uses both, "For he maketh

*Erich Sauer, *In the Arena of Faith* (London: Paternoster, 1955), p. 99.

sore, and bindeth up: he woundeth, and his hands make whole" (Job 5:18). When the necessary work has been done in the soul, He is ready to heal. To grant healing before that point is reached would defeat the purpose of the whole experience.

Evidently the psalmist wanted something more than healing. Not only was his soul badly shaken; it stood in real danger, probably of death itself. So he prays, "Return, O Lord, deliver [or, rescue] my soul: oh save me for thy mercies' sake" (Ps 6:4). He no longer pleads his weakness, but the Lord's mercies, or lovingkindnesses: "For in death there is no remembrance of thee: in the grave [sheol] who shall give thee thanks?" (v. 5).

It is amazing how fatalistic our prayers may become when we are out of communion with the Lord and have lost the joy of our salvation. All hope for the future is gone, and God Himself is the loser! "In the grave who shall give thee thanks?" And that came from one who, in a better state of soul could say, "Yea, though I walk through the valley of the shadow of death, I will fear no evil: for thou art with me" (Ps 23:4). No wonder the tears flowed freely, so much so that he made his "bed to swim," He wept till he actually lost his vision. "Mine eye is consumed because of grief" (Ps 6:7). But this, we note, he blames on his enemies. He does not blame the Lord for this. There is here none of the spirit of Naomi who complained upon her return to Bethlehem: "The Almighty hath dealt very bitterly with me" (Ru 1:20). On the contrary, he shouts, "Depart from me, all ye workers of iniquity; for the LORD hath heard the voice of my weeping" (Ps 6:8). Since he does not identify these enemies, they probably were people who were mocking him because of his continuing faith in the Lord in spite of his present plight. Recall how the chief priests, scribes, and elders mocked the Lord Jesus, saying, "He saved others; himself he can not save. If he be the King of Israel, let him now come down from the cross, and we will believe him. He trusted in God; let him deliver him now, if he will have him: for he said, I am the Son of God. The thieves also, which were crucified with him, cast the same in his teeth" (Mt 27:42-44). And what if He had come down? The cross would be the symbol of defeat instead of victory! At that time, it is true, He cried and was not heard (Ps 22:2). But before He concludes we hear Him saying, "Thou hast heard me from the horns of the unicorns" (v. 21).

In like manner, the psalmist could say, "The LORD hath heard the voice of my weeping. The LORD hath heard my supplication; the LORD will receive my prayer" (Ps 6:8-9). He neither resented nor despised the chastening of the Lord. And this peaceable fruit of righteousness is proof that he was exercised thereby.

So far as his enemies are concerned, he has the assurance that they will be dealt with in due time. According to a more literal translation, the last verse of this psalm should read, "All mine enemies shall be ashamed and tremble exceedingly; they will turn, they will be ashamed suddenly" (Ps 6:10).

No doubt there was much in the life of the psalmist with which his enemies could taunt him. But the Lord loved him. It was because He loved him that He chastened him. And what looked like anger and hot displeasure turns out to be an ardent love that will not let him go. "For he maketh sore, and bindeth up: he woundeth, and his hands make whole" (Job 5:18). If "we have had fathers of our flesh which corrected us, and we gave them reverence; shall we not much rather be in subjection unto the Father of spirits, and live? For they verily for a few days chastened us after their own pleasure; but he for our profit, that we might be partakers of his holiness" (Heb 12:9-10).

From the title of the psalm, we learn that it was to be sung to the accompaniment of "Neginoth," or stringed instruments. According to Gesenius, "upon Sheminith" denoted the lowest and gravest notes, as sung by men; the modern bass."

Since, for the most part, there is not a note of joy or praise in the psalm, we may well suppose that it was sung in a minor key. It may even yet be used by those who pass through the great tribulation. But we can also see how well suited it is for those who are being sorely tried in our own times as well. It is prophetic, but it is also truly contemporary.

MY ALL IN ALL

O blessed Lord, whose hand has led me on
    By paths no vulture's eye hath seen;
I thank Thee for each upward step, though rough,
    Though bare of brooks and pastures green;
For Thou wast there my All in All.

Yet, Lord, I thank Thee, too, for tears that cleansed,
  That purged mine eyes from dimming dross,
When I had wept till I could weep no more,
  And heavy seemed to me my cross,
Thou, Thou wast then my All in All.

And if the vale of deathly gloom I tread,
  With tears for drink, and grief for bread;
I'll know that Thou hast planned it so for me,
  That I have nothing now to dread,
For Thou art still my All in All.

And though the road ahead may still look steep,
  And rough the path that leads me home,
The perfect day for me has dawned, and soon
  Where every tear is dried, I'll come
To be with Thee, my All in All.*

CARL ARMERDING

*Reprinted by permission from the June 1946 issue of MOODY MONTHLY.

5

PSALM 7:1-5

Persecuted

FROM THE VERY BEGINNING, the course of Christianity was marked by persecutions and martyrdoms. No other of the faiths of mankind, religious or political, has had quite so extensive a record of violent and bitter opposition to its growth. This of course was predicted by the Lord Jesus who said to His disciples, "If they have persecuted me, they will also persecute you" (Jn 15:20). It was not long after the birth of our Lord that Joseph was warned in a dream to "Arise, and take the young child and his mother, and flee into Egypt, and be thou there until I bring thee word: for Herod will seek the young child to destroy him" (Mt 2:13).

In the very first paragraph of His Sermon on the Mount, the Lord said, "Blessed are they which are persecuted for righteousness' sake: for their's is the kingdom of heaven. Blessed are ye, when men shall revile you, and persecute you, and shall say all manner of evil against you falsely, for my sake, Rejoice, and be exceeding glad: for great is your reward in heaven: for so persecuted they the prophets which were before you" (Mt 5:10-12).

Those last words show that persecution is not peculiar to the Christian era. It began in the days of Cain and Abel when "Cain rose up against Abel his brother, and slew him" (Gen 4:8). "And wherefore slew he him? Because his own works were evil, and his brother's righteous" (1 Jn 3:12).

Speaking of Ishmael and Isaac, Paul says, "Then he that was born after the flesh persecuted him that was born after the Spirit, even so it is now" (Gal 4:29). And Stephen, as he was about to be martyred for Christ's sake, asked, "Which of the prophets have not your fathers persecuted? and they have slain them which shewed before of the coming of the Just One; of whom ye have been now the betrayers and murderers" (Ac 7:52).

David, the writer of Psalm 7, was in that line. And according to the title of the psalm, it was "Cush the Benjamite" who headed up the persecution. Saul, the first king of Israel, was also a Benjamite. Some commentators believe that "Cush" is a veiled reference to Saul. Be that as it may, the psalmist did not resort to an arm of flesh in dealing with his persecutor. He appealed to the LORD his God to save him from all them that were persecuting him, of whom Cush was the leader.

The intensity of the persecution is indicated in verse 2 where the psalmist says, "Lest he tear my soul like a lion, rending it in pieces, while there is none to deliver." Granting that the language here is highly poetic (the soul is not material like the body), it would seem that here he is referring to something worse than death, such as the torture inflicted on a victim without actually killing him. The horrible details of cruel and inhuman sufferings inflicted on Christians in the days of the Roman emperors, Nero to Diocletian, as well as in the times of the medieval and Spanish Inquisition, need not be repeated here. They would furnish us with many vivid illustrations of experiences similar to that of the psalmist.

In contrast to such awful persecution, it is beautiful to note the spirit of the psalmist. "O LORD my God, if I have done this; if there be iniquity in my hands; If I have rewarded evil unto him that was at peace with me; (yea, I have delivered him that without cause is mine enemy:) Let the enemy persecute my soul, and take it; yea, let him tread down my life upon the earth, and lay mine honour in the dust. Selah" (vv. 3-5).

Clearly, these words indicate that all the charges made against him were false. But his defense is not only negative; it is positive. "Yea, I have delivered him that without cause is mine enemy." On at least two occasions he had spared the life of Saul. When Abishai begged David to let him pin his enemy to the earth with his spear, David said, "Destroy him not: for who can stretch forth his hand against the LORD's anointed, and be guiltless? David said furthermore, As the LORD liveth, the LORD shall smite him; or his day shall come to die: or he shall descend into battle, and perish" (1 Sa 26:9-10). Thus he left his persecutor in the hands of the LORD his God.

Verses 3 and 4 of Psalm 7 suggest the case of another Benjamite, not as a persecutor (although he had been that) but as one who, like David, was experiencing persecution and that, of course, is the apostle Paul who, as he himself tells us, was "of the tribe of Benjamin" (Phil 3:5). Standing "at Caesar's judgment seat," many and grievous complaints were laid against him which his accusers could not prove. In his defense before Festus he said, "To the Jews have I done no wrong, as thou very well knowest. For if I be an offender, or have committed any thing worthy of death, I refuse not to die: but if there be one of these things where of these accuse me, no man may deliver me unto them. I appeal unto Caesar" (Ac 25:7-11).

In appealing to Caesar, perhaps Paul was not as spiritual as David who appealed to the LORD his God. But the circumstances were quite different. David was not being tried in some heathen court. He was being persecuted by a fellow Israelite. The LORD God was the judge. Paul was being tried in a Roman court, before a heathen judge. Being a Roman it was quite in order that he should appeal to Caesar. He could say, "I stand at Caesar's judgment seat, where I ought to be judged" (Ac 25:10). Even so, he could say with David, "If I be an offender . . . I refuse not to die."

In our own times it would not be difficult to find cases parallel to those of David and Paul. Men and women are still being persecuted, and even killed, because they are Christians. What the Communists are doing to Christians in China and other countries which they dominate is common knowledge. Even secular press agencies have taken note of this. But even under severe restrictions and persecution, the churches of mainland China survive!

In referring to those in other lands, let us also remember those who are being persecuted for Christ's sake right here in America. For all such, it must be a comfort to know that in all of their affliction, the Lord Himself is afflicted (Is 63:9). When Saul of Tarsus was persecuting the Christians, the Lord asked him, "Why persecutest thou me?" (Ac 9:4). And when Saul inquired, "Who art thou, Lord?" the Lord replied, "I am Jesus whom thou persecutest" (Ac 9:5).

In writing to those who were suffering in like manner, Peter said, "Beloved, think it not strange concerning the fiery trial which is to try you, as though some strange thing happened to you: But rejoice, inasmuch as ye are partakers of Christ's sufferings; that, when his glory shall be revealed, ye may be glad also with exceeding joy" (1 Pe 4:12-13).

In his very last letter, addressed to Timothy, Paul refers particularly to the persecutions he had endured for Christ's sake. "Yea, and all that will live godly in Christ Jesus shall suffer persecution" (2 Ti 3:12). The early Christians were no strangers to this, but they rejoiced that they were "counted worthy to suffer shame for his name" (Ac 5:41).

As one who knows from personal experience what it means to suffer for Christ's sake, I can bear witness to the fact that the Lord never seemed to be nearer, nor more precious than when another missionary and I were being stoned for His sake. "Wherefore let them that suffer according to the will of God commit the keeping of their souls to him in well doing, as unto a faithful Creator" (1 Pe 4:19).

> With joy we meditate the grace
>   Of God's High-Priest above;
> His heart is filled with tenderness,
>   His very name is Love.
>
> Touched with a sympathy within,
>   He knows our feeble frame;
> He knows what sorest trials mean,
>   For He has felt the same.
>
> But spotless, undefiled, and pure,
>   The great Redeemer stood.
> While Satan's fiery darts He bore,
>   And did resist to blood.
>
> He, in the days of feeble flesh,
>   Poured out His cries and tears,
> *And, though ascended, feels afresh*
>   *What ev'ry member bears.*
>
> Then boldly let our faith address
>   The throne of grace and power;
> We shall obtain deliv'ring grace
>   In ev'ry needed hour.
>
>   ISAAC WATTS

6

PSALM 11

"Flee as a Bird"

THE QUESTION which opens this psalm sounds so modern that it might have been written today. Indeed, many of the airlines' advertisements which we hear and see every day could be summed up in these very words, *"Flee as a bird,"* or *"Let's get away from it all."* And they make a strong appeal to any who may be looking for an escape from the strains and pressures of modern life.

That there are times when a way out is needed is not denied. But the Lord has made full provision for that. "No temptation [or trial] has come your way that is too hard for flesh and blood to bear. But God can be trusted not to allow you to suffer any temptation beyond your powers of endurance. He will see to it that every temptation has a way out, so that it will never be impossible for you to bear it" (1 Co 10:13, Phillips).

In the first verse of Psalm 11, the psalmist tells us what that way is. It is the way of trust, or faith. "In the LORD put I my trust," or, "In the LORD have I taken refuge." And this is so satisfying that he is surprised that anyone should suggest anything else. Hence the question, "How say ye to my soul, Flee as a bird to your mountain?" as if he were a hopeless fugitive.

The biographies of great men and women of faith show that no matter how desperate the situation, there was always a "way out." Existentialism may lead to "No Exit," but not so the way of faith. The psalmist makes no reference to any other way, even though he may, like so many of us, have tried something else. He was not merely trusting some thing, but some*one*.

That is what makes the life of faith distinctive. It begins when we trust Christ as our personal Saviour. "As many as received him, to them gave he power to become the sons of God, even to them that believe on his name" (Jn 1:12). One might be a Confucian without knowing Confucius, or a Moslem without knowing Mohammed. But the Christian can say, "We know that the Son of God is come, and hath given us an understanding, that we may know him that is true, and we are in him that is true, even in his Son Jesus Christ. This is the true God, and eternal life" (1 Jn 5:20).

The suggestion to flee is followed by a direct attack. "For, lo, the wicked bend their bow, they make ready their arrow upon the string, that they may privily [or, in darkness] shoot at the upright in heart" (Ps 11:2). This is developed in greater detail in Psalm 10:8-10. The book of Job contains a classic example of it. With the Lord's permission, Satan was allowed to do what he might to Job—short of taking his life—to prove his allegation that Job was not so spiritual after all. But Job held "fast his integrity" (Job 2:3). With "the shield of faith"—that is, the shield which faith takes—he was "able to quench all the fiery darts of the wicked" (Eph 6:16). The Lord was Job's shield, just as He was in the case of Abram (Gen 15:1).

But the enemy is resourceful. What he cannot achieve by direct attack he attempts with the weapon of discouragement, by way of supposition. "If the foundations be destroyed, what can the righteous do?" (Ps 11:3). Thank God, there is a foundation which cannot be destroyed. "For other foundation can no man lay than that is laid, which is Jesus Christ" (1 Co 3:11). Not even Satan can destroy that. So we may rightly sing, "On Christ the solid rock I stand, All other ground is sinking sand."

But the word here is in the plural, and it could be used figuratively to mean those who stand in a place of prominence or leadership, men who are looked upon as "pillars" (cf. Gal 2:9). We all know how the enemy seeks to destroy such in one way or another, with the object of destroying the faith of those who look up to them as spiritual leaders.

But there is another way of looking at these foundations. It has been suggested that they are the foundations "of the social order of society itself." Take the home, for example, which is often referred to as the foundation of society. In these days of broken homes, we may well wonder what has become of that foundation. Time was when such a tragedy was considered unlikely, if not impossible, among Christians. But it has overtaken us in alarming proportions.

Closely linked to this is the breakdown in morals. Situation ethics has actually become acceptable in many religious circles. With the abandonment of moral standards, another foundation has been destroyed. Similar observations could be made of our educational, political, and economic systems. The overall picture is enough to fill one with despair. And because of it, many are asking, "What can the righteous do?"

The answer to that question is found in Psalm 11:4. The psalmist does not look to any human or mundane source for help. He looks up, and with the eye of faith, he sees the Lord in His holy temple, enthroned in the heavens. In that vision two very wonderful things are brought together. To see the Lord in His holy temple suggests His priesthood. To see Him on His heavenly throne confirms His transcendent royalty. In other words, He is there as the priest after the order of Melchizedek. In the Mosaic economy, the office of priest and that of king were kept distinct. Any attempt to combine them met with severe punishment, as may be seen in the case of Uzziah, king of Judah (2 Ch 26:16-21).

But the one whom the psalmist saw does not belong to the Levitical priesthood.

> For it is evident that our Lord was descended from Judah, a tribe with reference to which Moses spoke nothing concerning priests. And this is clearer still, if another priest arises according to the likeness of Melchizedek, who has become such not on the basis of a law of physical requirement, but according to the power of an indestructible life. For it is witnessed of Him,
>
> > "THOU ART A PRIEST FOREVER
> > ACCORDING TO THE ORDER OF MELCHIZEDEK."
>
> And inasmuch as it was not without an oath (for they indeed became priests without an oath, but He with an oath through the One who said to Him,
>
> > "THE LORD HAS SWORN
> > AND WILL NOT CHANGE HIS MIND,
> > 'THOU ART A PRIEST FOREVER' ");
>
> so much the more also Jesus has become the guarantee of a better covenant. Hence also He is able to save forever those who draw

near to God through Him, since He always lives to make intercession for them (Heb 7:14-17, 20-22, 25, NASB).

This last is something of which many Christians are not aware, and yet without it, none of us could live the Christian life in a world like this without being overcome.

My father made this truth of Christ's priesthood real to me when I was a young Christian. I had invited a friend to attend one of our meetings held in a store which had been made into a place of worship—a converted store for converted people. But my friend informed me that he could not attend any of our meetings unless I should first attend service in his place of worship. With my father's permission, I did just that.

I had never attended a service like that one before. The interior of the building was beautiful, and I was overawed at the sight of priests clad in their splendid robes. There was no preaching, but I noticed that the people in the congregation responded occasionally to something the priest had said. When it was all over, I was filled with wonder and amazement.

Having fulfilled the condition laid down by my friend's parents, I reminded him of his promise to attend one of our services. True to his word, he went with me the following Sunday evening. The service, as usual, was very simple. There were a couple of hymns, sung a cappella, followed by prayer for God's blessing on His word. The message of the evening was delivered by a godly layman. A brief prayer brought the service to a close.

On our way home I asked my friend what he thought about the service. His reply was that he supposed it was all right, "But," said he, "you don't have a priest." In his church, the priest was a very important individual. No wonder he missed him in our humble place of worship. I made no reply.

When I got home my father asked me about Bill's reaction to the service. I told him that Bill said, "You don't have a priest."

"And we don't," said I.

Dad assured me that we do have a priest. To prove it, he reached for his Bible, turned to Hebrews 4:14, and read, "We have a great high priest, that is passed into the heavens, Jesus the Son of God," emphasizing the adjectives *great* and *high*. But I was curious to know what He does for us. In replying to that, Dad turned to

Hebrews 7:25 and read, "he ever liveth to make intercession for" us.

I told Dad I did not know the full meaning of the word *intercession,* so he explained that it means that He is always praying for us. I have never forgotten that lesson.

When I saw my friend again, I was all ready for him. In my little New Testament I showed him the verse which my father had pointed out to me. Strangely enough, he asked the same question that I asked: "What does He do for you?"

When I explained to him that our Lord always lives to pray for us, his remark was, "It must be wonderful to have someone praying for you all the time." And it is. And because it is, we have no need to flee to our mountain or to be discouraged because the foundations of society have been destroyed.

The Lord may try us (Ps 11:5) as He did Abraham, but He knows exactly how much we can take. "He knoweth the way that I take: when he hath tried me, I shall come forth as gold" (Job 23:10). The time will come when He will deal with those who have harrassed His people. "His eyes behold, his eyelids try, the children of men" (Ps 11:4). The horrible fate which awaits all such enemies is vividly depicted in verse 6. Of one thing we can be sure, "The righteous LORD loveth righteousness" (v. 7). "We are sure that the judgment of God is according to truth" (Ro 2:2). Meanwhile we who trust in Him have the comfort of knowing that His eye is ever upon us for good. "His countenance doth behold the upright" (Ps 11:7).

> Jesus, before Thy face we fall—
> Our Lord, our life, our hope, our all!
> For we have nowhere else to flee—
> No sanctuary, Lord, but Thee!
>
> In Thee we ev'ry glory view,
> Of safety, strength, and beauty too:
> 'Tis all our rest and peace to see
> Our sanctuary, Lord, in Thee!
>
> Whatever foes or fears betide,
> In Thy blest presence we may hide;
> And while we rest our souls in Thee,
> Thou wilt our sanctuary be!

Through time, with all its changing scenes,
Through all the grief that intervenes,
This shall support each fainting heart—
That Thou our sanctuary art!

SAMUEL MEDLEY

7

PSALM 12

"The Godly Man Ceaseth"

IN THE OPENING VERSE of Psalm 12, David discloses the pressure he feels from ungodly people, by saying, "Help, LORD; for the godly man ceaseth," or, "I'm the only one left who really loves God." These words remind me of a similar complaint made by the prophet Elijah when he fled from Jezebel and took refuge in a cave. There the Lord asked him twice, "What doest thou here, Elijah?" And twice he replied, "I have been very jealous for the LORD God of hosts: for the children of Israel have forsaken thy covenant, thrown down thine altars, and slain thy prophets with the sword; and I, even I only, am left; and they seek my life, to take it away" (1 Ki 19:10, 14).

These are the words of a great man in a time of deep distress. Only those who have been in similar circumstances can fully appreciate his feelings. They are not the words of a proud man but of one who mourns because he is, so far as he knows, the only one left who is faithful to the Lord and His covenant. Unknown to him there were seven thousand in Israel who had not bowed their knee to Baal nor kissed his image (1 Ki 19:18). What an encouragement they might have been to the prophet had they been as faithful as he!

The psalmist's reaction is similar to that of Elijah, but their circumstances had one major contrast: Elijah fled the wicked followers of Baal, and David remained where he was, seemingly surrounded by ungodly men.

David goes on in Psalm 12:2 to describe the people he sees around him. "They speak vanity every one with his neighbour: with flattering lips and with a double heart do they speak." Speaking vanity (or, emptiness) with one's neighbor may sound innocent enough in itself, but it does not stop there. "Sweet nothings" often expand into flattery and even duplicity. Flattery is insincere or excessive praise, and sometimes Christians are guilty of it.

A fine Christian came up to me once after I had preached at the small chapel which he attended, with the remark that he had never heard anything finer in his life and that he was sure it could never be excelled. I spoke again at the evening service, and I wondered what he would say after that, since he was so profuse in his praise of the morning address. But he was equal to the occasion. Said he, "I did not think it could be done, but this evening you really outdid yourself."

How does one respond to a remark like that? The best I could do was to credit him with a desire to be appreciative. Harsh as it may sound, one would prefer the honesty of the preacher who conducted the funeral of an unbeliever and concluded by saying, "I hope this brother's soul is where I expect it ain't."

Careless praise and idle chatter will eventually lead to the situation Paul described when he wrote that "in the latter times some shall depart from the faith, giving heed to seducing spirits, and doctrines of devils; speaking lies in hypocrisy; having their conscience seared with a hot iron" (1 Ti 4:1-2).

The psalmist traces all of this to a "double heart," or "a heart and a heart," as it is in the original. Our Lord said, "Out of the heart of men, proceed evil thoughts, adulteries, fornications, murders, Thefts, covetousness, wickedness, deceit, lasciviousness, an evil eye, blasphemy, pride, foolishness" (Mk 7:21-22). Truly, "The heart is deceitful above all things, and desperately wicked: who can know it?" (Jer 17:9).

The evil reaches its climax in verse 4 of Psalm 12, where those who speak proud things say, "With our tongue will we prevail; our lips are our own: who is lord over us?" That sounds like the Pharaoh of Moses' day who also said, "Who is the LORD, that I should obey his voice and let Israel go? I know not the LORD, neither will I let Israel go" (Ex 5:2). But his proud lips were later silenced. And, "The LORD shall cut off all flattering lips, and the tongue that speaketh proud things" (v. 3).

Such were the things that caused the psalmist to cry out, "Help, LORD." Not only did he witness the vanishing of the faithful, but he faced the problem of how to live a godly life in a generation

like that. The answer to his prayer is seen in verse 5. "For the
oppression of the poor, for the sighing of the needy, now will I
arise, saith the LORD."

The question may be asked, "Why wait so long before doing
something about it?" There are times when, like James and John,
we feel like calling down fire from heaven to consume the ungodly,
only to be reminded that we know not what manner of spirit we
are of (Lk 9:54-55). Sometimes the divine patience lingers long
because the wickedness has not reached the limit (cf. Gen 15:16)
and because God is longsuffering, not willing that any should perish.

But He is fully aware of the oppression of the poor and the
sighing of the needy. And when He says, "Now will I arise" we
know that there will be no more delay. And the first thing that He
does is to "set him in safety from him that puffeth at him" (Ps 12:
5). He does not tell us how He will do this. It could be by removing the saint from the scene altogether. That is exactly what will
occur when the Lord comes to receive His own to Himself that
where He is there we may be also (John 14:1-3).

But according to verse 7 of our psalm, the Lord preserves His
own without removing them from the world. When our Lord
prayed for His own He said, "I pray not that thou shouldest take
them out of the world, but that thou shouldest keep them from the
evil" (Jn 17:15).

Not only are believers constantly being tried by the world, God's
own Word is often put to the test to determine its validity. But the
psalmist assures us, "The words of the LORD are pure words: as
silver tried in a furnace of the earth, purified seven times" (Ps
12:6).

The "furnace of earth" suggests the place where the tests take
place, right here where you and I live. And the "seven times" indicates that His words have been tested completely and thoroughly.
Indeed, the more they are tried the clearer they become to us. And
their keeping power is confirmed so that we may say, "By the word
of thy lips I have kept me from the paths of the destroyer" (Ps 17:
4). Yes, even though "the wicked walk on every side when the
vilest men are exalted," and even though "the godly man ceaseth"
and "the faithful fail from among the children of men," the Lord
will preserve His own forever.

8

PSALM 13

Forgotten!

EVERY ONCE in a while, some social worker calls our attention to the fact that there are thousands of men and women in hospitals, rest homes, and similar institutions, who feel completely forgotten by their friends and relatives (even though some of the latter actually help to support these shut-ins), because they never visit or write to them. Of course, some of the institutions referred to have chaplains who are a great blessing to those under their care. But the human heart has longings that only those next of kin can satisfy. To be forgotten by such is distressing indeed.

But to be forgotten by God is something else again. And the question naturally arises, "How can the omniscient one ever forget any who live and move and have their being in Him?" (cf. Ac 17: 28). The answer to that question depends on the meaning of the word *forget* as it occurs in the first verse of our psalm. In the latter part of the verse, the psalmist expresses it in other words: "How long wilt thou hide thy face from me?" This is a feature of Hebrew poetry known as parallelism, or a repetition of ideas. Thus we learn that to forget in this context means to hide the face from one.

An outstanding example of this is seen at Calvary, when "from the sixth hour there was darkness over all the land unto the ninth hour. And about the ninth hour Jesus cried with a loud voice, saying . . . My God, my God, why hast thou forsaken me?" (Mt 27: 45-46). God was hiding His face, as it were, from the one "who his own self bare our sins in his own body on the tree" (1 Pe 2:24). He suffered what we deserved to suffer. As our blessed Substitute He "endured the cross, despising the shame" (Heb 12:2). And

43

because of that we can sing, "The Father's face of radiant grace shines now in light on me."

The psalmist does not tell us what it was that caused the Lord to hide His face from him. It might have been some "earthborn cloud." But I am inclined to believe that it was some fault on the part of the psalmist himself. Every child of God knows only too well what that is like. Failure to observe a quiet time is a common cause of broken fellowship. Neglect of the Word of God and of prayer is bound to bring a cloud between us and our Lord. Then too, it could be because of some sin in our lives.

Because of their sins, the Lord had to say to His ancient people, "Behold, I, even I, will utterly forget you, and I will forsake you, and the city that I gave you and your fathers, and cast you out of my presence" (Jer 23:39). But from the pen of the same prophet we have the assurance that "the Lord will not cast off for ever: But though he cause grief, yet will he have compassion according to the multitude of his mercies. For he doth not afflict willingly nor grieve the children of men" (Lam 3:31-33).

In all of this, note that the psalmist does not charge the Lord with injustice, but he is impatient. "How long wilt thou forget me, O LORD? for ever?" Surely not. When "Zion said, The LORD hath forsaken me, and my Lord hath forgotten me," He replied by saying, "Can a woman forget her sucking child, that she should not have compassion on the son of her womb? yea, they may forget, yet will I not forget thee. Behold, I have graven thee upon the palms of my hands" (Is 49:14-16). A further illustration of the Lord keeping those who are His own is that He said, "My sheep hear my voice, and I know them, and they follow me: and I give unto them eternal life; and they shall never perish, neither shall any man pluck them out of my hand. My Father, which gave them me, is greater than all; and no man is able to pluck them out of my Father's hand" (Jn 10:27-29).

In spite of such assurances from the Word of God, some of us still are not convinced that we are loved with an everlasting love (Jer 31:3). Instead of turning directly to the one who loves us, we take counsel in our soul, and as a result have sorrow in our heart daily. No doubt there are times when introspection is both necessary and salutary. But unless this is followed by a look of faith to the Lord Himself, we are bound to be miserable. Only as we look unto Him are our faces "lightened," or radiant (Ps 34:5).

To further complicate matters, the psalmist mentions an enemy who is exalted over him (Ps 13:2). Perhaps someone was taking advantage of his low state of soul and was making use of it to torment him even more.

The fact that he had taken counsel in his soul (v. 2) suggests that he tried to find some way out of his difficulty. We have all tried this method again and again. We may even have thought that by doing something nice He would overlook that which led to our forgetting Him, just as one might bring home a gift to an offended loved one, instead of humbly offering the appropriate apology or confession.

Verse 3 marks a turn in the right direction. The psalmist no longer asks, "How long?" Nor does he seek within his own soul for a solution to his problem. Instead he prays that his eyes may be lightened.

He longs for the dawn of a new day in his soul, "lest I sleep the sleep of death" (v. 3). The word here rendered "sleep" is not the usual word employed in the historical books as a euphemism for physical death. It is the same word as that used in Genesis 2:21 when we are told that "the LORD God caused a deep sleep to fall upon Adam, and he slept." Its primary meaning is slack or languid, reminding us of Paul's exhortation, "Let us not sleep, as do others; but let us watch and be sober" (1 Th 5:6). In other words, what the psalmist dreaded was not physical death so much as indifference, or spiritual death. It is easy to become stoical, and indifferent to trial, thus losing the blessing the Lord may have in it for us. Evidently the psalmist is aware of this danger and prays that it may be averted.

The second thing the psalmist dreads is defeat, "Lest mine enemy say, I have prevailed against him" (Ps 13:4). Nothing is quite so frustrating as defeat. And to have to listen to one's enemy say, "I have prevailed against him," would only make matters worse. Thank God we do not have to go down to defeat. "Nay, in all these things we are more than conquerors through him that loved us" (Ro 8:37).

Perhaps "the unkindest cut of all" is to be ridiculed when we slip. Said David, "And those that trouble me rejoice when I am moved." Thank God, even that can be prevented. "I have set the

Lord always before me: because he is at my right hand, I shall not be moved" (Ps 16:8). Occupation with Christ will keep us from slipping.

The psalm closes with a most delightful triad—trust, joy, and singing. "I have trusted in thy mercy [or, lovingkindness]; my heart shall rejoice in thy salvation. I will sing unto the Lord, because he hath dealt bountifully with me" (vv. 5-6).

> Sun of my soul, Thou Saviour dear,
> It is not night if Thou be near;
> O may no earthborn cloud arise
> To hide Thee from Thy servant's eyes.
>
> JOHN KEBLE

9

PSALM 14

"No God"

PSALM 14:1 says, "The fool hath said in his heart, There is no God." It would be quite easy for those who claim to be believers in God to exclude themselves from this verse. And yet, a good many who unquestionably believe in God often behave as if He did not exist! We would be shocked to hear them say so in so many words. But then the fool referred to here did not say so either. That is, he did not say so out loud. He said in his heart, "No God." What a man says in his heart is what he thinks, and what he thinks determines what he is, "For as he thinketh in his heart, so is he" (Pr 23:7).

For our present purpose, however, we shall limit the application of these words to those who have no hope and are without God in the world (Eph 2:12). To give our study a frame of reference, let us suppose we are in a large courtroom, one large enough to accommodate the whole human race. The trial begins with a grievous charge against those who by word or deed, or both, have expressed their antipathy to the one in whom all live and move and have their being (Ac 17:28).

Since what a man thinks is not acceptable evidence in an ordinary court of law, it may be argued that the plaintiff has no case. But this court is different. The judge is none other than the Judge of all the earth (Gen 18:25), and "He knoweth the secrets of the heart" (Ps 44:21). The prosecuting attorney—and we use that title reverently—is the one to whom the Lord Jesus referred when He said that "He will reprove [or, convict] the world of sin, and of righteousness, and of judgment" (Jn 16:8), the Holy Spirit. In making His charge, the Prosecutor does not stop with what a man thinks; He also declares what man is and what he does. "There is none righteous, no, not one." These very words are cited by the apostle Paul in Romans 3:10 and applied to all men everywhere, having proved that both Jews and Gentiles are all under sin. Such a universal application may well give us pause. But we are living in days when our news reporters confirm every word. The corrupt character and abominable works of the defendants are the fruit of their negative thinking about God. "There is none that seeketh after God" (Ro 3:11).

But these charges are not accepted without investigation. In Psalm 14:2 we read, "The LORD looked down from heaven upon the children of men, to see if there were any that did understand, and seek God." Note that He did not look for perfection. But it is after His manner of doing things to make an investigation. We may be quite sure that God knew, without inquiring, that Adam and Eve had partaken of the forbidden fruit in the garden of Eden. He did not have to come down to learn about that. But the fact that He came down to investigate shows how just He is in all of His dealings with men. Before He brought the flood upon the world, He came down to see what the children of men were doing. "And GOD saw that the wickedness of man was great in the earth, and that every imagination of the thoughts of his heart was only evil continually" (Gen 6:5). Notice again the direct connection between man's thoughts and his deeds.

Before God halted the building of the city and tower of Babel, He "came down to see the city and the tower, which the children of men builded" (Gen 11:5). In judgment He confounded their language so that they might not understand one another's speech. "So the LORD scattered them abroad from thence upon the face of all the earth: and they left off to build the city" (Gen 11:8).

Before He destroyed Sodom and Gomorrah, He also made an investigation (see Gen 18 and 19). And before He poured out His judgments upon the land of Egypt, He said, "I have surely seen the affliction of my people which are in Egypt, and have heard their cry by reason of their taskmasters; for I know their sorrows; And I am come down to deliver them" (Ex 3:7-8).

So we could go on through the Scriptures to show that God does not judge men without an impartial investigation. And His object in so doing is to see "if there were any that did understand, and seek God," a gracious objective indeed.

In view of all this, the findings of the court are most disappointing. "They are all gone aside, they are all together become filthy: there is none that doeth good, no, not one" (Ps 14:3). There are no exceptions. All that was charged in the beginning of this envisioned trial is found to be true. As we have seen, all of this is applied to our generation by the Holy Spirit in Romans 3. And in spite of man's attempts to improve things, they keep getting worse. If these findings were those of some extremist, we might dismiss them without hesitation. But they are the words of Him who is holy and omniscient. And they cannot be denied.

In discussing these matters I have been told that some consideration should be given those who are trying to live up to the Sermon on the Mount, for example. My reply to such is that they had better try something easy. The Ten Commandments would be a lot easier to keep than the Sermon on the Mount. One could conceivably keep nine of the Ten Commandments without doing anything. The only commandment which requires positive action is the one which says, "Honour thy father and thy mother." And that, by the way, is the first commandment with promise (Eph 6:2).

According to the Sermon on the Mount, even the thought of evil condemns one (Mt 5:28). That being so, and human nature being what it is, we can see how utterly impossible it would be for one to gain divine acceptance by living up to it. If salvation depended on that, our case would be hopeless. And if it were possible to live up to it from this day forward, that would not atone for the past.

But someone may ask, What about extenuating circumstances? And what about those who are too ignorant to know the difference between right and wrong? Verse 4 of our psalm deals with that problem. "Have all the workers of iniquity no knowledge?" Are they really that ignorant? Is it because they are not educated? These questions hardly allow for a negative answer in a country like ours. The leading opponents of God's Word are, and generally have been, those who pride themselves on their intellectual attainments and superiority. And they are also most intolerant. They literally fulfill the charge that they "eat up my people as they eat bread, and call not upon the LORD" (Ps 14:4). Of course, this statement does not mean that they are cannibals. The language is figurative. Because they can overcome a simple believer in an argument, they boast of their superiority and shame, or confound, the counsel of the poor, "because the LORD is his refuge" (Ps 14:6).

They do not call upon the Lord in prayer, but mock those who do. The story is told of a Quaker preacher who was opposed by a skeptic who said he did not believe that there is a God who answers prayer. The Quaker quietly asked him, "Friend, dost thou pray?"

"No, not I,'" said the skeptic. "Then what dost thou know about it?" asked the preacher. Answered prayer is a powerful apologetic.

It is not lack of knowledge that makes infidels. Scripture declares, "That which may be known of God is manifest in them; for God hath shewed it unto them" (Ro 1:19). "For since the creation of the world His invisible attributes, His eternal power and divine nature, have been clearly seen, being understood through what has been made, so that they are without excuse" (Ro 1:20, NASB).

It is the realization of this when they face a Christless eternity which causes the "great fear" mentioned in Psalm 14:5. Having ministered to the sick and dying for some ten years in a TB sanatorium, I had plenty of opportunity to see how men die. To sit by the bedside of a Christian as he passed into the presence of the Lord was a sacred experience. But in those years, I also had the sad experience of witnessing the last moments of some who professed no faith in God or His Word. Earlier in life, one of them had "shamed the counsel of the poor because the LORD is his refuge." He departed this life in a manner which left no doubt as to his awful destiny.

Psalm 14 does not close without showing us how such an end may be averted. In keeping with the frame of reference which we have been using in our study, I would suggest that in the last verse we may hear the accused casting himself upon the mercy of the court. "Oh that the salvation of Israel were come out of Zion!" (v. 7) expresses the longing of one who realizes that there is hope in no other. And the salvation for which he longs is not merely some*thing* but some*one*. Salvation does not come separately from a Saviour.

Among those who ardently longed for the coming of this one was an old man by the name of Simeon. The Holy Spirit revealed to him "that he should not see death, before he had seen the

Lord's Christ . . . and when the parents brought in the child Jesus . . . then took he him up in his arms, and blessed God, and said, Lord, now lettest thou thy servant depart in peace, according to thy word: for mine eyes have seen thy salvation, Which thou hast prepared before the face of all people; A light to lighten the Gentiles, and the glory of thy people Israel" (Lk 2:26-32).

In the light of the context, it is clear that the salvation which Simeon saw was none other than "the Lord's Christ." He has not yet come out of Zion—as He will one day—but He did come to Bethlehem, "the city of David," where He was hailed as "a Saviour, which is Christ the Lord" (Lk 2:11), a condemned sinner's only hope. And He said, "I solemnly assure you that the man who hears what I have to say and believes in the one who has sent me has eternal life. He does not have to face judgment; he has already passed from death into life" (Jn 5:24, Phillips).

10

PSALM 20

"The Day of Trouble"

THIS PSALM gives a good example of what it means to intercede for another. While not addressed directly to the Lord, it is essentially a prayer in the same sense that the benediction (Num 6:24-26) is a prayer uttered on behalf of another.

The role of an intercessor is a solemn one. In 1 Timothy 2, intercession is listed as one of four things which are of prime importance. If we think of these things as successive steps which culminate in thanksgiving, it would appear that prayer is not complete until it takes the form of intercession. Intercession has been defined as a "personal and confiding intercourse with God on the part of one who is able to approach Him."* It is essentially altru-

*J. N. Darby,

istic, a holy service rendered on behalf of others. He who intercedes is not concerned for the time being with his own need but altogether with the need of another. Accordingly, it is not until we come to the last verse of this psalm that we hear the intercessors include themselves in their prayer.

Intercession is something more than "saying" prayers. It has to do with specific persons who have specific needs. This is evident from the very opening words of the psalm, even though it assumes that the one prayed for also prays for himself. "The LORD hear thee in the day of trouble." The literal meaning of the word *trouble* here is tightness, or as we might say in our vernacular, "in a jam." It does not refer to trouble in general—the world is full of that—but to some particularly trying experience. Since it is not described or defined, we may make our own application.

We note that the "name of the God of Jacob" is invoked here. And it is most appropriate. It was used by the Lord Himself at the burning bush when He revealed Himself to Moses as the deliverer of His people, saying, "Thus shalt thou say unto the children of Israel, The LORD God of your fathers, the God of Abraham, the God of Isaac, and the God of Jacob, hath sent me unto you: this is my name for ever, and this is my memorial unto all generations" (Ex 3:15). It may well be that this verse was in the minds of these intercessors when they said, "The name of the God of Jacob defend [or, protect] thee."

But that is only one of three things which are brought together here. He not only defends, He sends help and He strengthens. The help He sends is from the sanctuary, and the strength issues out of Zion. The sanctuary suggests the temple, or the holy place; whereas Zion suggests His throne (Ps 2:6). Thus two more precious aspects of the Lord Jesus are illustrated here: His priesthood and His royalty. I refer here to His Melchisedec priesthood, "Wherefore he is able also to save them to the uttermost that come unto God by him, seeing he ever liveth to make intercession for them" (Heb 7:25).

If the source of help counts for anything, and it does, then this must be help indeed. It is not the kind of help described in verse 7 of Psalm 20, where we are told, "Some trust in chariots, and some in horses." Those who trust in chariots and horses "are brought down and fallen: but we are risen, and stand upright" (v. 8).

In verse 3 we learn something of the spiritual life of the one for whom prayer is offered. Mention is made of the offerings and the burnt sacrifice which he had made, in much the same way that the "alabaster box of very precious ointment" which a woman poured on the Lord's head as He sat at meat (Mt 26:7), is made a matter of permanent record.

The offerings referred to here are described in Leviticus 2. They were made of fine flour and oil, with frankincense sprinkled on them. These offerings are quite generally looked upon as types of the holy life of our Lord. The burnt sacrifice mentioned later in the same verse is described in Leviticus 1. It is a type of the sacrificial death of the Lord. Both of these offerings were known as sweet savour offerings (Lev 1:17; 2:2). They were offered voluntarily as an expression of the worship and devotion of the offerer. From this we may learn something of the saintly character of the one being prayed for in Psalm 20. And because of this we may rightly infer that the trouble mentioned in the beginning was not the result of some sin he had committed.

Although we Christians do not bring meal offerings and animal sacrifices, it is our privilege as members of "an holy priesthood, to offer up spiritual sacrifices, acceptable to God by Jesus Christ" (1 Pe 2:5). "By him therefore let us offer the sacrifice of praise to God continually, that is, the fruit of our lips giving thanks to his name" (Heb 13:15).

After a brief pause (Selah, v. 3), the prayer continues: "Grant thee according to thine own heart, and fulfil all thy counsel." The expression, "according to thine heart" is interesting. We are accustomed to think, and rightly so, of God answering our prayers according to His riches in glory by Christ Jesus (Phil 4:19). But this takes into account the heart's desire, such as the apostle Paul had when he wrote, "Brethren, my heart's desire and prayer to God for Israel is, that they might be saved" (Ro 10:1). The counsel could refer to some plan or project he may have had in mind, supposedly for the glory of the Lord.

The intercessors are so sure of a favorable answer that they are bold to say, "We will rejoice in thy salvation, and in the name of our God we will set up our banners" (Ps 20:5). They expect nothing short of complete victory, concluding with one more comprehensive wish: "The LORD fulfil all thy petitions."

So far we have not heard from him for whom prayer is being made. But in verse 6, we hear him exclaim, "Now know I that the LORD saveth his anointed; he will hear from his holy heaven with the saving strength of his right hand." No doubt the "anointed" referred to here is the Messiah. But by God's sovereign grace, we may also apply this to ourselves, because "He which stablisheth us with you in Christ, and hath anointed us, is God; Who hath also sealed us, and given the earnest of the Spirit in our hearts" (2 Co 1:21-22). And "as he is, so are we in this world" (1 Jn 4:17). And He has said, "Call upon me in the day of trouble: I will deliver thee, and thou shalt glorify me" (Ps 50:15). And faith replies, "In the day of my trouble I will call upon thee: for thou wilt answer me" (Ps 86:7). Psalm 20 ends with a plea from the intercessors for themselves as well as the one for whom they are interceding. "Save, LORD: let the king hear us when we call." Amen.

11

PSALM 25

"Let Me Not Be Ashamed"

IT IS RECORDED of Ezra that he was ashamed to ask of the king a band of soldiers and horsemen to help against the enemy because they had spoken unto the king saying, "The hand of our God is upon all them for good that seek him; but his power and his wrath is against all them that forsake him" (Ezra 8:22). It is quite possible that the psalmist had made a similar assertion, because he says in verse 2 of this psalm, "O my God, I trust in thee . . . let not mine enemies triumph over me."

In the next verse he broadens his request to include all who wait on the Lord. It would be bad enough for the psalmist's enemies to overcome him, but for them to triumph over him would be even worse. Such a defeat would make him doubly ashamed, especially if he had openly declared his faith in the Lord.

To wait on the Lord means to expect something from Him, with a high degree of certainty. In the words of St. Paul, "According to my earnest expectation and my hope." Such expectation usually looks for an affirmative answer. But some, because the Lord does not always answer as and when they would like, become so cautious that they refuse to be positive about anything which has to do with the promises of God.

In that connection there is something to be learned from the literal meaning of the word *shame* as it occurs in our text. It means to turn pale, or, to lose the glow. And yet, to be "fervent in spirit" (Ro 12:11) or to "maintain the spiritual glow" as Moffatt renders it, is expected of believers in the one who "is able to do exceeding abundantly above all that we ask or think, according to the power that worketh in us" (Eph 3:20).

Evidently the psalmist dreaded losing the glow. In verses 20 and 21 of Psalm 25, he prays, "O keep my soul, and deliver me: let me not be ashamed; for I put my trust in thee. Let integrity and uprightness preserve me; for I wait on thee." This is a healthy sign. Even before one's words or deeds indicate backsliding, the disappearance of the glow which accompanies a vibrant testimony for the Lord is a symptom which no amount of makeup can cover up. Therefore, not to lose the glow would indicate that the psalmist had no wish to backslide whatever.

Verses 4 and 5 show how this glow is restored and maintained. The process begins with prayer. "Shew me thy ways, O LORD; teach me thy paths." It has been suggested that God's ways are His general directions, whereas His paths are the details. To this the psalmist adds the request for personal guidance and instruction: "Lead me in thy truth, and teach me." No one can maintain the spiritual glow apart from the truth of God. His Word is not only a lamp to our feet and a light unto our path, but the entrance of His Word gives light within as well (Ps 119:105, 130). And to have His personal leadership is even more wonderful. To be taught by Him is a privilege indeed. This makes our Christian faith unique.

In pleading for this, the psalmist uses a double argument. First, "Thou art the God of my salvation" (Ps 25:5). And *salvation* here means more than the salvation of the soul. It includes that constant preservation and deliverance that we need all through life. St. Paul used the word in that sense in writing to the Philippians. "For I know that this shall turn to my salvation through your prayer, and the supply of the Spirit of Jesus Christ, According to my earnest expectation and my hope, that in nothing I shall be ashamed, but that with all boldness, as always, so now also Christ shall be magnified in my body, whether it be by life, or by death. For to me to live is Christ, and to die is gain" (Phil 1:19-21).

The second argument which the psalmist uses is, "On thee do I wait all the day" (Ps 25:5). Here again David and Paul speak the same language. With them, communion with God was something more than a brief devotional. They lived a life of continual dependence on the Lord. This does not mean, of course, that they spent their days in some lonely cell counting their prayer beads. Like the two on their way to Emmaus, their hearts must have burned while He talked with them by the way, and while He opened to them the Scriptures (Lk 24:32). Thus they maintained the glow.

The verses which follow give details with which every child of God is familiar. These include memories that both bless and burn (vv. 6-7). In asking to be remembered, the psalmist does not plead anything that he may have said or done, but rather "according to thy mercy remember me for thy goodness' sake, O LORD." He does not for one moment doubt the goodness and uprightness of the Lord (v. 8). And because He is good and upright, He takes us just as we are, "sinners in the way," and teaches us. This is the starting point of a truly spiritual life. Only He could make anything out of such unpromising material. Therefore each one He finds must exclaim with Elihu, "Behold, God exalteth by his power: who teacheth like him?" (Job 36:22).

"The meek will he guide in judgment: and the meek will he teach his way" (Ps 25:9). And in all of this, He is the blessed example. Says He, "Take my yoke upon you, and learn of me; for I am meek and lowly in heart: and ye shall find rest unto your souls. For my yoke is easy, and my burden is light" (Mt 11:29-30). As we do this, we discover that "all the paths of the LORD are mercy and truth unto such as keep his covenant and his testimonies" (Ps 25:10). That there will be failure is anticipated. Hence the prayer, "For thy name's sake, O LORD, pardon mine iniquity; for it is great" (v. 11). And we know that "if we confess our sins, he is faithful and just to forgive us our sins, and to cleanse us from all unrighteousness" (1 Jn 1:9).

In verse 12 of our psalm, we come to that which is basic to a life of holiness and joy in the Lord. It is the fear of the Lord, or reverential awe; not the loss of courage, or terror. We may excuse some who, because of immaturity, talk about the Lord in a crude and irreverent manner. But as we "grow in grace, and in the knowledge of our Lord and Saviour Jesus Christ" (2 Pe 3:18), we learn to give Him the honor that is His due. And He has said, "Them that honour me I will honour" (1 Sa 2:30).

The ways in which He honors those who fear Him are seen in Psalm 25:12-14. First of all, He honors them by teaching them "in the way that he shall choose." To be taught by Him *in* the way implies that He will accompany them in that way. This is the answer to the prayer recorded in verses 4 and 5. And the "exceeding abundantly above" is seen in verse 13: "His soul shall dwell at ease [or, in prosperity]." It is the Old Testament equivalent of what we have already seen in Matthew 11:29, "Ye shall find rest unto your souls." And who does not long for that, in days like these? The possibility of it has yet to be discovered by most of us. But the steps that lead to it are as plain as can be.

What is probably the greatest honor of all is seen in verse 14. "The secret of the LORD is with them that fear him; and he will shew them his covenant." "Think of being, as it were, the bosom friends of God, to whom He can speak freely of what is hidden from the rest of men! Here surely is complete blessing. Herein is communion perfected."* No wonder the psalmist says, "Mine eyes are ever toward the LORD" (v. 15). The apostle Paul carries this a point further when he says, "But we all, with unveiled face beholding as in a mirror the glory of the Lord are being transformed into the same image from glory to glory, just as from the Lord, the Spirit" (2 Co 3:18, NASB). Those who do this will never be ashamed, or grow pale. They will experience what the psalmist expressed in another psalm: "They looked unto him, and were lightened: and their faces were not ashamed" (Ps 34:5). Only thus will we be able to "maintain the spiritual glow."

"And now, little children, abide in him; that, when he shall appear, we may have confidence, and not be ashamed before him at his coming" (1 Jn 2:28).

---

*F. W. Grant, *The Numerical Bible,* vol. 3, *The Psalms* (Neptune, N.J.: Loizeaux, 1897), p. 120.

12

PSALM 26

"I Shall Not Slide"

DAVID KNEW from experience what it means to stand in slippery places. His sin with Bathsheba has left its stain on the story of his life to this day. It all began at the time when the kings went forth to battle, but "David tarried still at Jerusalem. And it came to pass in an eveningtide, that David arose from off his bed, and walked upon the roof of the king's house: and from the roof he saw a woman washing herself; and the woman was very beautiful to look upon" (2 Sa 11:1-2). The rest of the story needs no repetition. David slipped into sin, the results of which hounded him till the day of his death. Considering the number of wives he had (2 Sa 3:2-5), his sin is entirely without excuse.

In bright contrast to this is the story of Joseph who "was a goodly person, and well favoured. And it came to pass after these things, that his master's wife cast her eyes upon Joseph; and she said, Lie with me. But he refused" (Gen 39:6-8). If ever a man was in a slippery place, it was Joseph. But he did not slide.

Whether the psalmist wrote this psalm before or after his grievous fall need not detain us now, except to say that if he had lived up to what he wrote here, Psalm 51 would never have been written. In any case, with the example of Joseph before him, he could not plead ignorance nor lack of warning. The law under which he lived specifically forbade the sins of adultery and murder. He committed both. And yet, when he was restored he promised to "teach transgressors" God's ways (Ps 51:13).

The very thought of sliding or slipping suggests danger and helplessness. In such a situation one naturally lays hold upon any help that may be available. But even apart from such help, if "the law of his God is in his heart; none of his steps shall slide" (Ps 37:

31). Evidently Joseph obeyed the voice of God in his heart long before the written law was given. He is a good example of what the psalmist claimed when he said, "I have trusted also in the LORD; therefore I shall not slide" (Ps 26:1). Joseph must have known what it means to walk by faith. By God's grace all who walk by faith may say, "I shall not slide."

In the previous psalm, 25, David prayed, "Let integrity and uprightness preserve me; for I wait on thee" (v. 21). And what is that but walking by faith? When Abimelech, the king of Gerar, sent and took Sarah, the wife of Abraham, the Lord withheld him from sinning because of the integrity of his heart and the innocency of his hands (Gen 20:1-6). Like Joseph, he also lived before the law of Moses was given. It is reasonable to suppose that David was acquainted with this fact of history.

All of these things may well make us wonder about the request he makes in verse 2 of Psalm 26. "Examine me, O LORD, and prove me; try my reins and my heart." The reins here are understood to be the seat of the feelings or passions. With complete abandon, he prays the Lord to search him through and through. And that, we may be sure, would be something other than a Freudian psychoanalysis! In direct connection with this, he says, "Thy lovingkindness is before mine eyes: and I have walked in thy truth" (Ps 26:3). It was this that enabled him to walk in God's truth, in complete separation from vain persons, dissemblers, and evil doers. Even so, he realized that his own hands needed cleansing as he prepared to draw near to the altar of God. "Who shall ascend into the hill of the LORD? or who shall stand in his holy place? He that hath clean hands, and a pure heart" (Ps 24:3-4).

The altar here quite properly suggests the cross of Christ of which it is the Old Testament symbol. In compassing, or going around it, one could view it from every side. The various sacrifices offered thereon foreshadowed the sacrifice of Christ in its varied aspects. In preparation for the sacrifice, one washed his hands in innocence. When Moses erected the tabernacle in the wilderness "he set the laver between the tent of the congregation and the altar, and put water there, to wash withal. And Moses and Aaron and his sons washed their hands and their feet thereat: When they went into the tent of the congregation, and when they came near unto the altar, they washed; as the LORD commanded Moses" (Ex 40:30-

32). The spiritual significance of this is seen in Ephesians 5:25-27 where we are told that "Christ also loved the church, and gave himself for it; That he might sanctify and cleanse it with the washing of water by the word, That he might present it to himself a glorious church, not having spot, or wrinkle, or any such thing; but that it should be holy and without blemish."

In the New Testament we also have symbols of the death of Christ with this difference, among others, that whereas the Old Testament symbols pointed forward to Christ, the Lord's Supper looks back to what He did at Calvary. In preparation for its proper observance, one must examine himself. "For as often as ye eat this bread, and drink this cup, ye do shew the Lord's death till he come. But let a man examine himself, and so let him eat of that bread, and drink of that cup" (1 Co 11:26, 28). As the scenes of Gethsemane and Calvary are thus brought before us, we sometimes sing,

> On Calv'ry we've adoring stood
> And gazed on that wondrous cross,
> Where the holy, spotless Lamb of God
> Was slain in His love for us

> J. G. DECK

In this way we too may be said to "compass the altar."

The psalmist continues his prayer-wish in Psalm 26:7. "That I may publish with the voice of thanksgiving, and tell of all thy wondrous works." Such good things are not to be kept to ourselves. They are to be shared with others. As we do this we are not apt to slide. A path of service may be rough at times, but it is not slippery. "The path of the just is as the shining light, that shineth more and more unto the perfect day" (Pr 4:18). And it leads to the Father's house. In view of that, we can say with the psalmist, "LORD, I have loved the habitation of thy house, and the place where thine honour dwelleth" (Ps 26:8). And that was written before the temple was built. Never doubting his ultimate arrival in God's house, he can say, "But as for me, I will walk in mine integrity: redeem me, and be merciful unto me. My foot standeth in an even place: in the congregations will I bless the LORD" (vv. 11-12).

"Thus saith the LORD of hosts; If thou wilt walk in my ways . . .

I will give thee places to walk among those that stand by" (Zec 3:7). Based on this promise, we can voice assuredly with the psalmist, "Therefore I shall not slide."

13

PSALM 28

"Be Not Silent to Me"

THE DESIRE to be heard is common to all of us. Who of us has not complained at some time or other, "He (she) will not listen to me." Of course there is "a time to keep silence" (Ec 3:7), and happy is the man who knows when to observe it. When our Lord "was accused of the chief priests and elders, he answered nothing. Then said Pilate unto him, Hearest thou not how many things they witness against thee? And he answered him to never a word" (Mt 27:12-14a).

In the psalm now before us, the psalmist seems to fear that God might ignore him. Just why he feared that he does not say. But he does tell us what it would be like if the Lord did not hear him. He would "become like them that go down into the pit" (Ps 28:1). The awful meaning of that is brought out elsewhere in Scripture. It is written of Lucifer that he should "be brought down to hell, to the sides of the pit" (Is 14:15).

In verses 3 and 5 of Psalm 28, we are told what kind of people go to the pit. They are those who "speak peace to their neighbors, but mischief is in their hearts." "They regard not the works of their LORD, nor the operation of his hands." Their judgment will be "according to their deeds, and according to the wickedness of their endeavours" (v. 4). The psalmist rightly dreads becoming like them. In that regard he manifests a sensitivity which we would do well to emulate. We get so used to the evil all around us that we do not think much, if at all, of the awful destiny of "them that go down into the pit."

It is to such people that the Lord says,

63

Because I have called, and ye refused; I have stretched out my hand, and no man regarded; But ye have set at naught all my counsel, and would none of my reproof: I will also laugh at your calamity; I will mock when your fear cometh; When your fear cometh as desolation, and your destruction cometh as a whirlwind; when distress and anguish cometh upon you. Then shall they call upon me, but I will not answer; they shall seek me early, but they shall not find me: For that they hated knowledge, and did not choose the fear of the LORD: They would none of my counsel: they despised all my reproof. Therefore shall they eat of the fruit of their own way, and be filled with their own devices (Pr 1:24-31).

The psalmist is not in their class. Therefore he can sing, "Blessed be the LORD, because he hath heard the voice of my supplications. The LORD is my strength and my shield." The Lord gave him "exceeding abundantly above all" that he asked. The Lord was not only David's strength but his shield as well, the double blessing of ability and protection.

Evidently a transition in mood happens in less time than it takes to tell it. Before he was discouraged to the point of despair. Now he can say, "My heart trusted in him, and I am helped: therefore my heart greatly rejoiceth; and with my song will I praise him" (Ps 28:7). Any apparent delay in responding to the cry of His servant must have been for some good reason, unknown to us, but fully known to Him whose wisdom is unsearchable "and his ways past finding out" (Ro 11:33).

There was one thing, even in his despair, which the psalmist did not forget. The LORD was his rock. He had a good foundation. And that means a lot when all around your soul gives way. With his feet firmly planted on this solid foundation, David lifted up his hands to God's holy oracle. According to 1 Kings 6:16, this was "the most holy place." It was there that the Lord promised Moses that He would meet with him and *speak* with him (Ex 25:22, NASB). That is why it is called the oracle. The oracle in the tabernacle was a type of the heavenly oracle (Heb 9:24).

As Christians, it is our privilege to "enter into the holiest by the blood of Jesus, By a new and living way, which he hath consecrated for us, through the veil, that is to say, his flesh; And having an high priest over the house of God; let us draw near with a true heart in full assurance of faith" (Heb 10:19-22). There, at His throne of grace we shall obtain mercy and find grace to help in time of need (Heb 4:16). In other words, we shall be heard; He will not be silent toward us.

And there we too shall find that the Lord is our strength and "the saving strength of his anointed." The saving strength mentioned here is literally a stronghold of salvations. These salvations are those repeated deliverances which He grants us as we move through a world that is contrary to us. The word *anointed,* which is in the singular here, is thought by many to refer to the Messiah. *Messiah* and *Anointed* are synonyms. Their New Testament equivalent is *Christ.* But since the Lord's people are referred to as His anointed ones (2 Co 1:21), we can see how this might refer to us as well.

The prayer that closes this psalm stands in vivid contrast to the request voiced in verse 4, where the Lord is asked to give "the workers of iniquity" "their desert." Here it is not a question of desert, but of grace. Those for whom prayer is made here are His people, His inheritance, and, by inference, His sheep. Each of these concepts is pregnant with meaning.

First, His people are those whom He has saved "from their sins" (Mt 1:21), and those whom He continues to save, or deliver, as we have seen.

Second, they are His inheritance. As such they are His by right because He brought them forth "out of the iron furnace, even out of Egypt, to be unto him a people of inheritance" (Deu 4:20; 9:29).

Third, they "are his people, and the sheep of his pasture" (Ps 100:3). And because He is their shepherd, they shall not want (Ps 23:1).

Finally, to "lift them up for ever" (Ps 28:9) will be a fitting climax to their earthly pilgrimage. Then He who "carried them all the days of old" (Is 63:9) will bring them safely to "the house of the LORD for ever" (Ps 23:6).

Before our Lord left this world, He promised that He would come again and receive us unto Himself, that where He is, there we may be also (Jn 14:3). Generations of Christians have prayed for the fulfillment of that promise; "Even so, come, Lord Jesus" (Rev 22:20). To that prayer, He has been silent all these years. However, we are also promised that we must wait "for yet a little while, and he that shall come will come, and will not tarry" (Heb 10:37).

Then, no longer silent, He "himself shall descend from heaven with a shout, with the voice of the archangel, and with the trump of God: and the dead in Christ shall rise first: Then we which are alive and remain shall be caught up together with them in the clouds, to meet the Lord in the air: and so shall we ever be with the Lord. Wherefore comfort one another with these words" (1 Th 4:16-18).

14

PSALM 30

Mourning Turned into Dancing

ACCORDING TO THE TITLE of this psalm, "A Psalm and Song at the dedication of the house of David," it was written for the dedication of a house. Whether this was David's house or some other may be a moot question. It could hardly refer to the temple, because David did not build it, much less dedicate it. Of course he may have written this by way of anticipation, but I do not think that the psalm as a whole supports that.

A dedication, as a rule, marks the completion of a building's construction and the beginning of its occupation. According to Deuteronomy 20:5, the dedication of a new house was important enough to warrant a soldier's return from the battlefront, "lest he die in the battle, and another man dedicate it." The dedication of the temple in Solomon's day was accompanied by "a sacrifice of twenty and two thousand oxen, and an hundred and twenty thousand sheep: so the king and all the people dedicated the house of God" (2 Ch 7:5). The Jewish feast of Hanukkah, observed in December, commemorates the rededication of the temple after it had been defiled by Antiochus of Syria, in the days of the Maccabees.

From verses 1-3 of Psalm 30, we conjecture that the building of the house, like the rebuilding of Jerusalem and its walls in the days of Ezra and Nehemiah, was not without opposition so strong that it not only depressed David, but threatened his life as well. Those who build for the glory of God are bound to meet with opposition from him "whose name in the Hebrew tongue is Abaddon [destroyer], but in the Greek tongue hath his name Apollyon" (Rev 9:11). But God's builders have Him as their strong ally. That is why the psalmist could sing, "I will extol thee, O LORD; for

thou hast lifted me up, and hast not made my foes to rejoice over
me" (Ps 30:1). Evidently he had sunk so low that self-help was
of no avail. But the Lord lifted, or drew, him up.

By what means He lifted him up, we are not told. Figuratively
this could refer to an elevation of spirit out of a state of depression,
such as that Paul experienced when "God, that comforteth those
that are cast down, comforted us by the coming of Titus" (2 Co
7:6). Then too in answer to his cry, he was healed of whatever
hurt he may have received in his struggle with his foes. The Lord's
servants must not only be builders, they must also be warriors, with
a tool in one hand and a weapon in the other (Neh 4:15-18). Of
course, the weapons of our warfare are not carnal but "mighty
through God to the pulling down of strong holds" (2 Co 10:4).

Apparently the psalmist risked his life in this enterprise, for he
says, "O LORD, thou hast brought up my soul from the grave
[Sheol]: thou hast kept me alive, that I should not go down to the
pit" (Ps 30:3). Like Paul, he had the sentence of death in himself, that he should not trust in himself, but in God who raises the
dead (2 Co 1:9).

In calling upon others to join him in singing unto the Lord and
to give thanks at the remembrance of His holiness, David makes
certain statements which lead me to believe that he had boasted as
if his final success were due to his own strength. In his prosperity
he had said, "I shall never be moved" (Ps 30:6). Many another
has said the same. But, "Let him that thinketh he standeth take
heed lest he fall" (1 Co 10:12).

Nothing grieves the Lord more than our pride. It even arouses
His anger. But, "His anger endureth but a moment; in his favour
is life," for the penitent one. Thus, "weeping may endure for a
night, but joy cometh in the morning" (Ps 30:5). The Preacher
tells us, "Sorrow is better than laughter: for by the sadness of the
countenance the heart is made better" (Ec 7:3).

There are times when the Lord has to hide His face, times when
He can not look upon us with pleasure and approval. The psalmist
was sensitive to that. As a result, he was troubled when the Lord
hid His face. I fear that many of God's children have become so
accustomed to the absence of the light of His countenance that they
never miss it. Not so the psalmist. He was so desirous of it that
he even argued saying, "What profit is there in my blood, when I

go down to the pit? Shall the dust praise thee? shall it declare thy truth? Hear, O LORD, and have mercy upon me: LORD, be thou my helper" (Ps 30:9-10).

From these words we may get some idea of the deep exercise of soul that the psalmist passed through till he learned that it was the Lord who by His favor made his "mountain to stand strong." That lesson is not easily learned, because we are so prone to trust in our own strength. We all need the exhortation which Paul gave to Timothy, "Thou therefore, my son, be strong in the grace that is in Christ Jesus" (2 Ti 2:1). And again, "Be strong in the Lord, and in the power of his might" (Eph 6:10).

Then, instead of mourning over a lack of power, we shall experience a transmutation that only God can make. I use the word *transmutation* advisedly here, because what follows is something more than rehabilitation or restoration to a previous effective state. It is akin to what the medieval alchemists sought for, as they tried to transmute base metals into gold. What the psalmist experienced is more wonderful than that. The divine Alchemist had turned his mourning into dancing.

Alas, Jeremiah had to lament over the exact opposite of that. "The joy of our heart is ceased; our dance is turned into mourning" (Lam 5:15). And that could be said of much of human experience today. "For we know that the whole creation groaneth and travaileth in pain together until now" (Ro 8:22). Thank God the day is coming when He who came "to proclaim the acceptable year of the LORD" will come again "to comfort all that mourn; To appoint unto them that mourn in Zion, to give unto them beauty for ashes, the oil of joy for mourning, the garment of praise for the spirit of heaviness" (Is 61:2, 3).

In similar vein the psalmist said, "Thou hast put off my sackcloth, and girded me with gladness" (Ps 30:11). This is not the same as the exchange of which we read in Zechariah 3:4, where Joshua is stripped of his filthy garments and clothed with a "change of raiment." Neither is it the same as that which the prodigal experienced when he returned from the far off country (Lk 15:22). This is that of which the Lord Jesus spoke when He was about to leave His disciples: "Verily, verily, I say unto you, That ye shall weep and lament, but the world shall rejoice: and ye shall be sorrowful, but your sorrow shall be turned into joy" (Jn 16:20).

"To the end that my glory may sing praise to thee, and not be silent. O LORD my God, I will give thanks unto thee for ever" (Ps 30:12). In this way, the psalm closes as it begins, with a note of praise. But in between occur the cries for help (vv. 2, 8). In these major and minor tonalities, we perceive a combination of melodies suggestive of counterpoint. But in that day when "the tabernacle of God is with men . . . God shall wipe away all tears from their eyes; and there shall be no more death, neither sorrow, nor crying, neither shall there be any more pain: for the former things are passed away" (Rev 21:3, 4). "As well the singers as the players on instruments shall be there" (Ps 87:7), singing and playing under the personal direction of the chief Musician.

High, in the Father's house above,
  Our mansion is prepared;
There is the home, the rest we love,
  And there our bright reward.

With Him we love, in spotless white,
  In glory we shall shine;
His blissful presence our delight,
  In love and joy divine.

All taint of sin shall be removed,
  All evil done away;
And we shall dwell with God's Beloved,
  Through God's eternal day.

                                        J. G. DECK

15

PSALM 31

"Pull Me Out of the Net"

THIS PSALM reminds me of a cloudy day, during which the sunshine breaks through occasionally, finally ending in a glorious sunset. Notes of pessimism mingle with notes of hope and optimism, denoting an experience that is so typically human that we instinctively indentify ourselves with the writer.

Because of the striking similarity between the first part of verse 13 and Jeremiah 20:10, some have concluded that the prophet must have written the psalm. But the title attributes it to David. And the experiences here are so common that any one of us might have said the same. Who has not found himself caught in a net, as it were, at some time or other?

It has been pointed out that our enemy, the devil, uses one of two possible methods to destroy us. Sometimes he comes as "a roaring lion . . . seeking whom he may devour" (1 Pe 5:8). At some other time, he may come as "an angel of light" (2 Co 11:14) to beguile us, as he did Eve in the Garden of Eden. But we are "not ignorant of his devices" (2 Co 2:11), nor of his wiles, or methods, according to the original of Ephesians 6:11.

Actually there is no good reason why we should be caught in Satan's net. "Surely in vain the net is spread in the eyes of every thing that hath a wing" (Pr 1:17, margin, Oxford ed.). We often sing, "Sweet hour of prayer, Thy wings shall my petitions bear . . . And oft escaped the tempter's snare, By thy return, sweet hour of prayer." How little some of us use those wings! When Samson was caught in the net, he had no one to blame but himself. Likewise David, before his fall. The same may be said of many today who know all about the sad effects of drug abuse and yet get hooked.

71

The natural law is immutable. "Be not deceived; God is not
mocked: for whatsoever a man soweth, that shall he also reap.
For he that soweth to his flesh shall of the flesh reap corruption;
but he that soweth to the Spirit shall of the Spirit reap life everlasting" (Gal 6:7-8). Happy is the man who knows when he is
caught, so that he may turn to the only one who can deliver him.

It appears that the psalmist had missed the right way somewhere
along the line, for he prays, "For thy name's sake lead me, and
guide me" (Ps 31:3). Then in verse 6, he refers to "lying vanities"
which may well have been some of the "devices" the enemy used
to entangle him. As a result of this, he seems to have lost his vision
also, for he says, "Mine eye is consumed with grief" (v. 9). Indeed, his "life is spent with grief" and his years with sighing (v.
10). What wasted years they must have been! But in all honesty
he takes the blame when he says, "My strength faileth because of
mine iniquity, and my bones are consumed" (v. 10). Things had
come to such a sorry pass that he was a reproach among his enemies
and especially among his neighbors. Even his looks must have
changed for the worse, for he says that he was a fear to his acquaint-
ance and those who saw him fled from him (v. 11). Worst of all,
he was "forgotten as a dead man out of mind." No one even cared
to write his epitaph. He was "like a broken vessel" (v. 12) fit only
for the dump.

Such are the reflections of one who realizes that he has been
trapped by Satan. But, thank God, there is one who does not forget
His erring child who has been caught in "the net."

In the beginning of the psalm, David had turned to Him and
prayed that he might not be ashamed and that he might be delivered,
not only righteously but speedily (vv. 1-2). He was one of the
redeemed (v. 5), and as such he could commit his spirit into the
Redeemer's hand. His hand is not "shortened at all, that it cannot
redeem" (Is 50:2), even though we may have sold ourselves for
nought (Is 52:3).

Verse 14 of Psalm 31 marks a turning point. In simple faith,
the psalmist says, "But I trusted in thee, O LORD: I said, Thou art
my God." This is the third time that he mentions his trust, or faith
(vv. 1, 6). This trust enables him to say, "My times are in thy
hand" (v. 15). His "times" would comprehend the whole of his
lifetime (cf. Ec 3:1-8) and all the vicissitudes of life. We are apt

to associate our good times with the Lord and the evil times with the devil. But the psalmist makes no distinction here; childhood, youth, adulthood, and old age are all included. According to Dan Crawford, author of *Thinking Black*, if you were to quote this to an African, you would have to translate, "All my life's whys and whens and wheres and wherefores are in God's hand."

The fact that our "times" are in God's hand suggests control as well as security (Jn 10:28-29). It may also suggest direction. David had had some bad times, as we have seen. But in and through them all, the mighty hand of God was in complete control. And He was making all things work together for good, as we shall see. God will deliver David from the hand of his enemies and those that persecute him because His hand is stronger than theirs. But the psalmist wants more than deliverance. He yearns for a break in the cloud which had temporarily hidden God's face from him. "Make thy face to shine upon thy servant" (Ps 31:15), he pleads. But this is the blessed effect of spending time in the presence of the Lord, as witness Moses, whose face shone after he had spent forty days in His presence (see Ex 34:28-29). Stephen's face shone as "the face of an angel" as he stood before the Sanhedrin, just before he was put to death (Ac 6:15). And such may be our experience as we behold, as in a mirror, the glory of the Lord (2 Co 3:18). Such was the ardent desire of the psalmist.

Apparently that prayer was answered, because in Psalm 31:19, he bursts forth into praise: "Oh how great is thy goodness, which thou hast laid up for them that fear thee; which thou hast wrought for them that trust in thee before the sons of men!" It is the goodness of God that leads men to repentance (Ro 2:4). And how great must be the reserves, for he speaks of this as *laid up* for those that fear the Lord. It was specially wrought for them. The Lord actually labored to produce it. Such is the force of the word *wrought* here.

I cannot think of a better verse to connect with this than John 17:4, where our Lord says to His Father, "I have finished the work which thou gavest me to do." No wonder the psalmist said, "How great is thy goodness!" While it is true that all may avail themselves of this, here it is especially for those who fear (or, reverence) Him and for those who trust in Him. Such will not be caught in the tempter's net, for He will hide them in the secret of His presence from the pride of man and keep them secretly in His "pavilion from the strife of tongues," or, the slander of those who may seek their ruin.

Real spiritual progress may be noted here, because in Psalm 31:21, the psalmist breaks forth in worship: "Blessed be the LORD: for he hath shewed me his marvellous kindness in a strong city." From the dreadful captivity of the "net" he has been transported to the "strong city," freed and secure. This is his final destination, a description of which may be seen in Revelation 21:10-27. The New Jerusalem is not only strong, it is beautiful because "Strength and beauty are in his sanctuary" (Ps 96:6).

At home and at rest, the psalmist may now reflect upon his past when he said in his haste, "I am cut off from before thine eyes: nevertheless thou heardest the voice of my supplications when I cried unto thee" (Ps 31:22).

After his restoration, he can strengthen his brethren, saying, "O love the LORD, all ye his saints: for the LORD preserveth the faithful, and plentifully rewardeth the proud doer." It is quite possible that he was referring to himself as a "proud doer" because "Pride goeth before destruction, and an haughty spirit before a fall" (Pr 16:18). But now, fully restored, he can say, "Be of good courage, and he shall strengthen your heart, all ye that hope in the LORD" (Ps 31:24).

This brings to mind what has been called our Lord's favorite text: "Be of good cheer." This He said to a helpless paralytic and similarly to the woman who touched the hem of His garment and was made whole (Mt 9:2, 22). He spoke these same words as He drew near to the terrified disciples battling the storm: "Be of good cheer; it is I; be not afraid" (Mt 14:27). And on the point of leaving His own before returning to heaven, He said, "In the world ye shall have tribulation: but be of good cheer; I have overcome the world" (Jn 16:33). Yes, even after He went to heaven, He spoke these same words to His servant Paul when He stood by him one night and said, "Be of good cheer, Paul: for as thou hast testified of me in Jerusalem, so must thou bear witness also at Rome" (Ac 23:11). Therefore, "Be of good courage . . . all ye that hope in the LORD." Your present situation may be desperate indeed, but "He is able to deliver thee."

Our times are in Thy hand,
Father, we wish them there,
Our life, our soul, our all, we leave
Entirely to Thy care.

Our times are in Thy hand,
Whatever they may be,
Pleasing or painful, dark or bright,
As best may seem to Thee.

Our times are in Thy hand,
Why should we doubt or fear?
A Father's hand will never cause
His child a needless tear.

Our times are in Thy hand,
Jesus the crucified!
The hand our many sins had pierced
Is now our Guard and Guide.

Our times are in Thy hand,
Jesus the Advocate!
Nor can that hand be stretched in vain
For us to supplicate.

Our times are in Thy hand;
We'd always trust in Thee,
Till we have left this weary land,
And all Thy glory see.

W. F. LLOYD

16

PSALM 36

Man at His Worst, God at His Best

IN THIS BEAUTIFUL PSALM, we may trace two downward move-
ments: one is human, the other divine. It is on the dark background
of the former that the glory of the latter is displayed, in much the
same way that a jeweler might display some of his finest jewels on
a piece of black velvet. We get some examples of this in the Scriptures. The earliest promise of the Redeemer is given to us on the
dark background of man's first disobedience (Gen 3:15). The
promise of the virgin birth is the only bright spot in the history of
Ahaz, one of the wickedest kings Judah ever had (Is 7). And
when Paul would tell us of "the gospel of Christ which is the power
of God unto salvation," he gives it to us in a chapter which we
hesitate to discuss in its entirety.

The author of this psalm describes himself, not as a sociologist
or psychologist, but simply as "the servant of the LORD." The
word he used for *servant* is commonly used in referring to slaves.
It is the exact equivalent of the word which Paul often used to
describe himself. But, "He that is called in the Lord, being a servant, is the Lord's freeman" (1 Co 7:22). It is not likely that the
psalmist had any formal training as a psychologist, but he must
have been a keen observer of human behavior, which led him to
some very definite conclusions concerning it.

The idiom, "saith within my heart," is David's way of telling
us that he has done some reflective thinking on this subject. What
one says in his heart is what he thinks. And the matter which en-
gaged him was not some minor fault, but "the transgression of the
wicked" (Ps 36:1). And a transgression is something more serious
than a mistake or a sin of ignorance. It so happens that the first
sin man ever committed is called a transgression (Ro 5:14, 1 Ti

76

2:14). And that is nothing less than deliberate disobedience to a known command. And this begins, as Psalm 36:1 states, "because there is no fear of God before his eyes." He does not say that there is no knowledge of God. There was a time when all men knew God, but "when they knew God, they glorified him not as God, neither were thankful; but became vain in their imaginations, and their foolish heart was darkened" (Ro 1:21).

The next step down is self-flattery, "For he flattereth himself in his own eyes, until his inquity be found to be hateful" (Ps 36:2). "The unjust knoweth no shame" (Zep 3:5). And, "Out of the abundance of the heart the mouth speaketh" (Mt 12:34).

"The words of his mouth are iniquity and deceit" (Ps 36:3). The character of the stream reveals the nature of its source. The unregenerate heart "is deceitful above all things, and desperately wicked" (Jer 17:9).

But man was not always like this. The fact that "he hath left off to be wise, and to do good" (Ps 36:3) implies that there was a time when he was wise and his deeds good. The fall of man was not an accident. He deliberately "left off," that is, he stopped being wise and doing good, by an act of his own will. Furthermore, "He deviseth mischief upon his bed" (v. 4); he plots evil while he is at ease, free from the pressure of circumstances and the evil influence of others. He is an independent sinner.

"He setteth himself in a way that is not good." He determines his own course. And having lost all sense of moral values, "He abhorreth not evil" (v. 4). Thus that which began with a negative—"no fear of God before his eyes"—comes to a negative ending. Such are the findings of one who did some sober thinking on the problem of evil. And these are not mere hypotheses; they are facts. It is man at his worst.

But the psalmist does not stop here. As if replying to those who may ask, "Why doesn't God do something about it?" he goes on to show what God is doing about it. With him there may be a "problem of evil" but there is no "problem of God." As one who is acquainted with Him, he turns from all that man is to the only one who can solve the problem. And this He does, not as we might have expected, by inflicting well-deserved judgment, but by showing mercy, or lovingkindness, to those who had sinned so grievously against Him.

His lovingkindness has its source "in the heavens." To use a
popular phrase, "It's out of this world." "Every good gift and
every perfect gift is from above, and cometh down from the Father
of lights, with whom is no variableness, neither shadow of turning"
(Ja 1:17). We have considered man's downward course in the
first part of this psalm. Here we see another downward stream, but
how different in character! Like its divine Source, it "is first pure,
then peaceable, gentle, and easy to be intreated, full of mercy and
good fruits, without partiality, and without hypocrisy" (Ja 3:17).

God's loving-kindness manifests itself in three ways in this psalm:
in His faithfulness, His righteousness, and His judgments, or verdicts. In saying that His "faithfulness reacheth unto the clouds,"
I am persuaded that something other than physical clouds are meant
here. In Isaiah 44:22 He said, "I have blotted out, as a thick cloud,
thy transgressions, and, as a cloud, thy sins: return unto me; for I
have redeemed thee." In order to do that, He had to come down
(cf. Ex 3:8) into a world beclouded by sin and moral darkness,
to men who "loved darkness rather than light, because their deeds
were evil" (Jn 3:19). As the poet J. G. Deck wrote,

> Faithful amidst unfaithfulness,
> 'Mid darkness only light.

He came into the world to save sinners. Yes, His faithfulness
reached unto the clouds.

His lovingkindness manifests itself in righteousness also. It is
in the "gospel of Christ" that "the righteousness of God" "revealed
from faith to faith: as it is written, The just shall live by faith"
(Ro 1:16, 17). "To declare, I say, at this time his righteousness:
that he might be just, and the justifier of him which believeth in
Jesus" (Ro 3:26).

The psalmist compares God's righteousness to "the great mountains" (Ps 36:6) or, "the mountains of God" (ASV). Mountains
are the well-known symbol of stability and security. And because
of this, His judgments, or verdicts, are a great deep. They are
unfathomable.

> 'Tis the Cross of Christ the Saviour
>   Hath the Father's heart made known:
> All His grace to me the sinner,
>   Told in judgment on His Son!

> Measured by that cross, that darkness,
> Oh how deep God's love must be,
> Deep as were Christ's depths of anguish,
> Is the Father's love for me!

It is interesting to observe that both "man and beast" are mentioned in verse 6. Paul wrote, "The creature was made subject to vanity, not willingly, but by reason of him who hath subjected the same in hope. Because the creature itself also shall be delivered from the bondage of corruption into the glorious liberty of the children of God" (Ro 8:20-21).

Such a plan of redemption is bound to evoke praise, as well as acceptance. "How excellent is thy lovingkindness, O God! therefore the children of men put their trust under the shadow of thy wings." The provision of such a place of refuge is tantamount to an invitation to enter it that "we might have strong consolation, who have fled for refuge to lay hold upon the hope set before us: Which hope we have as an anchor of the soul, both sure and stedfast" (Heb 6:18-19).

But God's lovingkindness provides even more than a place of safety. Those who take refuge there "shall be abundantly satisfied with the fatness of thy house" (Ps 36:8). That is satisfaction with a surplus! It is nothing less than grace abounding (Ro 5:20). "That in the ages to come he might shew the exceeding riches of his grace in his kindness toward us through Christ Jesus" (Eph 2:7).

But the end is not yet. The psalmist continues, "Thou shalt make them drink of the river of thy pleasures. For with thee is the fountain of life: in thy light shall we see light" (Ps 36:8-9). Think of being made capable of enjoying what God enjoys! To drink of the river of His pleasures, to share His delight in His beloved Son (Mt 3:17) as well as His pleasure in saving souls (1 Co 1:21). And all of that from a fountain that never shall run dry.

The ardent desire for more of this loving-kindness is competent evidence of its soul-satisfying qualities. Therefore the prayer, "O continue thy lovingkindness unto them that know thee; and thy righteousness to the upright in heart" (Ps 36:10). That we "may be able to comprehend with all saints what is the breadth, and length, and depth, and height; And to know the love of Christ,

which passeth knowledge, that ye [we] might be filled with all the
fulness of God" (Eph 3:18-19).

But as long as we are in this world of sin, we shall have to be on
our guard. "The foot of pride" and "the hand of the wicked" are
ever with us here (Ps 36:11). "There are the workers of iniquity
fallen: they are cast down and shall not be able to rise" (v. 12).
And so a psalm which opens in a minor key, closes with the same.
But we recall that in Ezra's day those who "sang together by course
in praising and giving thanks to the Lord" overcame the noise of
weeping with their shouts of joy (Ezra 3:11-13).

> Awake my soul, to joyful days,
> And sing thy great Redeemer's praise;
> He justly claims a song from me,
> His loving-kindness, oh, how free!
>
> He saw me ruined by the fall,
> Yet loved me notwithstanding all;
> He saved me from my lost estate,
> His loving-kindness, oh, how great!
>
> Tho' num'rous hosts of mighty foes,
> Tho' earth and hell my way oppose,
> He safely leads my soul along,
> His loving-kindness, oh, how strong!
>
> When trouble, like a gloomy cloud,
> Has gathered thick and thundered loud,
> He near my soul has always stood,
> His loving-kindness, oh, how good!
>
> SAMUEL MEDLEY

17

PSALM 42

"Deep Calleth unto Deep"

THE TITLE of this meditation is taken from Psalm 42:7, because it seems to sum up what the psalm is all about. It is a heart cry from the creature to his Creator, an urgent call from a child to his heavenly Father. Man was made to have an ardent desire for God. The oft-quoted saying of St. Augustine expresses it well. "Thou hast made us for Thyself, and our heart is restless until it repose in Thee."

The thirst for God is one of the simplest apologetics there is for the existence of God. When the apostle Paul declared "the unknown God" to the Athenians, it was "that they should seek the Lord, if haply they might feel after him, and find him, though he be not far from every one of us: For in him we live, and move, and have our being" (Ac 17:27-28).

Likening himself to a hart (deer), the psalmist says, "As the hart panteth after the water brooks, so panteth my soul after thee, O God" (Ps 42:1). In likening himself to a wild but clean animal rather than to some human being, he could claim that which was quite natural, and not the result of teaching or discipline. There is only one who can satisfy such a thirst. "My soul thirsteth for God, for the living God" (v. 2a). No substitute or idol can meet that need. And he wants not only to hear about Him, he wants to come into His presence. "When shall I come and appear before God?" (v. 2b).

It certainly is not death and the judgment after death, that he longs for here. There is a sense in which we may appear before God at any time. We have but to draw near to Him, and He will draw near to us (Ja 4:8). Undoubtedly, he is here speaking of the presence of God as it may be experienced in the house of God. The psalmist's grief at being so far from the presence of the Lord was so intense that he wept day and night. Says he, "My tears have been my meat day and night, while they continually say unto me, Where is thy God?" (Ps 42:3). This question appears to have been put to him by those with whom he had gone "to the house of God, with the voice of joy and praise, with a multitude that kept holyday" (v. 4). They probably asked it in much the same way that we might say to a fellow Christian, "Where is your faith?" when he is tempted to doubt the promises of God or the love of God.

Memories of "the good old days," when we had sweet fellowship with other children of God, may well make us wonder whether we shall ever see the like again. Evidently the psalmist had hopes that such could be enjoyed again. Accordingly, he asks himself, "Why art thou cast down, O my soul? and why art thou disquieted in me? hope thou in God: for I shall yet praise him for the help of his countenance" (v. 5).

How well the psalmist knew the solution to his own problem! But knowing it is one thing; applying it is quite another. We all know something about that. But he is making progress. That this is so is indicated by the fact he turns from self to God. "O my God, my soul is cast down within me: therefore will I remember thee" (v. 6). To remember the happy fellowship enjoyed in other days is good. To remember God Himself is better.

The psalmist remembers Him in three different situations. First, "from the land of Jordan" (v. 6), where his forefathers terminated their wilderness journey and set foot on the soil of the promised land for the first time. What a day that was! The very thought of it should have lifted him out of his depression. I have known it to work that way in my own case when, like the psalmist, my soul was "cast down." To relive that blessed experience when I first knew the joy of salvation, gave me a lift indeed.

Then there are those mountaintop experiences that followed, as the psalmist viewed all He had done for them from "the Hermonites" or, the land of Hermon. To learn that He "hath blessed us with all spiritual blessings in heavenly places in Christ" (Eph 1:3)! What a discovery! It will take all eternity to explore it.

In contrast, we have a third situation, "the hill Mizar," or, "the little hill." This also is suggestive. It could mean that the psalmist sensed His presence with him in the little places. To be told then that "even the very hairs of your head are all numbered. Fear not therefore: ye are of more value than many sparrows" (Lk 12:7) was most reassuring. We are important to Him!

Still another thought suggests itself in connection with "the little hill." It was on a little hill that our blessed Lord humbled Himself and became obedient unto death, even the death of the cross (Phil 2:8). He was "despised and rejected of men; a man of sorrows, and acquainted with grief" (Is 53:3). But just before He went to the cross, He instituted the Lord's Supper by which we call Him to remembrance. If ever there was a time and place where deep called unto deep, it was at Calvary when He cried and said, "My God, my God, why hast thou forsaken me?" (Mt 27:46). And one of His last wishes was that we should remember Him there. In response to that we sometimes sing,

> We think of all the darkness
>   Which round Thy spirit pressed,
> Of all those waves and billows
>   Which rolled across Thy breast.
> Oh, there Thy grace unbounded
>   And perfect love we see;
> With joy and sorrow mingling,
>   We would remember Thee.

G. W. Frazer

It is interesting to note that the word for *deep* is the same as that used in Genesis 1:2, where we read that "darkness was upon the face of the deep," an apt picture of the sinner in his sins. But "God, who commanded the light to shine out of darkness, hath shined in our hearts, to give the light of the knowledge of the glory of God in the face of Jesus Christ" (2 Co 4:6). From this we learn that what God did on that first day is symbolic of what He did for us when He opened our eyes, "to turn them from darkness to light, and from the power of Satan unto God" (Ac 26:18). Well may we remember Him from "the hill Mizar," where in deep humiliation He suffered in that awful darkness in order that we might see the light.

In keeping with this, our psalmist says, "The LORD will command

his lovingkindness in the daytime, and in the night his song shall
be with me, and my prayer unto the God of my life" (Ps 42:8).
Each clause here calls for comment. The Lord will not only show
His loving-kindness in the daytime, He will command it. And
what He commands must come to pass. But that is for the daytime when all is bright. What about the night when all is dark?
Then "his song shall be with me." Paul and Silas illustrated that
when, at midnight in the prison at Philippi, they prayed and sang
praises unto God, and the prisoners heard them (Ac 16:25).

In a similar way, singing and praying are brought together here.
"His song shall be with me, and my prayer unto the God of my
life." This is a rather unusual name for God, and it is full of meaning. If God is the God of my life, it means that my life belongs to
Him in the same way that Paul's life belonged to Him, so that he
could say, "To me to live is Christ" (Phil 1:21).

But that sense of nearness to God makes it rather difficult to
explain what follows here. In one breath the psalmist says that
God is the God of his life, and in the next he says, "I will say unto
God my rock, Why hast thou forgotten me? why go I mourning
because of the oppression of the enemy?" (Ps 42:9). Perhaps it
was because the psalmist thought, as some of us have thought, that
once we became His by simple faith in the Lord Jesus, all of our
troubles would be at an end. Before we declared our faith in Christ,
there was no opposition from the world. But after we took our
stand with Him, we learned that because He has chosen us out of
the world the world hates us (Jn 15:19).

The oppression that comes from the world is crushing (v. 10,
ASV margin). "As with a sword in my bones, mine enemies
reproach me; while they say daily unto me, Where is thy God?"
(v. 10). They actually repeat the question put to him by those
with whom he went into the house of God, but with an entirely
different intent. Instead of reproof, it is used to reproach.

But having said all that he said he would say to God—he probably never really said it to Him—he turns again to his soul
with the question, "Why art thou cast down, O my soul? and why
art thou disquieted within me?" (v. 11a). Here it is not a question
of doubt or despair, but of self-reproof.

There is now no need for such depression. "Hope thou in God:
for I shall yet praise him, who is the health of my countenance,

and my God" (v. 11*b*). Hope in God will actually change one's looks. He will not have to use any makeup to make him look well. It will not be anything that he might put on, but a glow that shines from within.

> Not the prize of a weary struggle
> By one who is longing to shine,
> But the fruit of the contemplation
> Of the glory, Lord, that is thine.

"But we all, with unveiled face beholding as in a mirror the glory of the Lord, are transformed into the same image from glory to glory, even as from the Lord the Spirit" (2 Co 3:18, ASV). "They looked unto him, and were radiant; And their faces shall never be confounded" (Ps 34:5, ASV).

18

PSALM 46

Utter Confusion, Unutterable Peace

THIS PSALM is so contemporary in its description of the condition of the world in which we live that it might have been written yesterday. No reasons are given for the unrest described in Psalm 46, verses 2 and 3, but the symptoms are plain enough. Since God is not the author of confusion or disorder (1 Co 14:33), we dare not blame Him for this. It is man who is to blame for all of the pollution, confusion, and unrest which we see in the world today. In the beginning it was not so. When "the LORD God took the man, and put him into the garden of Eden to dress it and to keep it" (Gen 2:15), He put Adam into an environment that was immaculate and beautiful.

It is a common complaint that the world is in a mess. Some would even like to stop the world and get off, to use their own expression. Just what their next stop would be, they do not say. Neither do they mention the only one who can change things. Not so the psalmist. He begins his song by enunciating three things that God is to him and his fellows. "God is our refuge and strength, a very present help in trouble" (Ps 46:1). It is as our refuge that most of us got to know God in the first place, that "we might have a strong consolation, who have fled for refuge to lay hold upon the hope set before us: Which hope we have as an anchor of the soul, both sure and stedfast" (Heb 6:18-19).

He is not only our refuge, He is also our strength. Without Him we can do nothing. We "are kept by the power of God through faith unto salvation ready to be revealed in the last time" (1 Pe 1: 5). Therefore we need not hesitate to trust Him. In His incomparable prayer to His Father, Christ said, "Those that thou gavest me I have kept, and none of them is lost, but the son of perdition; that the scripture might be fulfilled" (Jn 17:12).

Besides all of this, He is "a very present help in trouble." He is easy to get at. That is more than can be said about some men, especially those in high places. Even some preachers are hard to reach. I once knew the pastor of a large church who told me that he had five secretaries. When I asked him why he needed so many secretaries, he told me that every Monday morning he was besieged by men and women who wanted to criticize his sermons of the day before. If secretary number one could not stop them, she would refer them to number two, and so on. By the time some of them finally reached number five, the pastor was conveniently out to lunch. Thank the Lord, He is not like that. "Let us therefore come boldly unto the throne of grace, that we may obtain mercy, and find grace to help in time of need" (Heb 4:16).

Having seen what God is to us and for us, we are prepared to consider the world and the mess it is in. Without such a preparation, we might well be afraid. But because of what He is, we too may say, "Therefore will not we fear, though the earth be removed, and though the mountains be carried into the midst of the sea: Though the waters thereof roar and be troubled, though the mountains shake with the swelling thereof" (Ps 46:2-3).

The interpretation of all this is given us in verse 6. "The heathen [or, nations] raged, the kingdoms were moved." "The wicked are like the troubled sea, when it cannot rest, whose waters cast up mire and dirt. There is no peace, saith my God, to the wicked" (Is 57:20-21). The mountains are symbols of governments, or kingdoms (cf. Zec 4:7).

In our psalm, we see these "mountains" carried into the midst, or, heart, of the sea. History—ancient as well as modern—furnishes us with numerous examples of empires and governments which have been overthrown. That such a calamity might overtake our own country is terrifying! A comparatively small group overthrew the Russian empire in 1904. That is something to think about. That is why the word *Selah* occurs at this point.

In direct contrast to the troubled scene we have just been considering, we are introduced to "a river, the streams whereof shall make glad the city of God, the holy place of the tabernacles of the most High" (Ps 46:4). A similar vision was granted the apostle

John when he was shown "a pure river of water of life, clear as crystal, proceeding out of the throne of God and of the Lamb" (Rev 22:1). There is no direct reference to the source of the river mentioned in our psalm, but we may be reasonably certain that it too proceeds out of the throne of God. Its main function is to make glad the city of God. Because God is in the midst of her—central to her life and government—she shall not be moved. God removes "those things that are shaken, as of things that are made, that those things which cannot be shaken remain. Wherefore we receiving a kingdom which cannot be moved, let us have grace, whereby we may serve God acceptably with reverence and godly fear: For our God is a consuming fire" (Heb 12:27-29).

Abraham, who lived some 2,000 years before Christ, "looked for a city which hath foundations, whose architect and builder is God" (Heb 11:10, Greek). Within its walls will be "the holy place of the tabernacles of the most High." The word for *tabernacles* occurs also in Psalm 84:1 where they are described as lovely, or, amiable. They are not the same, but certainly suggestive of the "many mansions" in the Father's house, of which our Lord Jesus spoke just before His passion. The fact that this city needs help (Ps 46:5) seems to indicate that this is not the eternal city mentioned in Revelation 21:1-4, even though they have much in common, because "God is in the midst of her; she shall not be moved: God shall help her and that right early," or, "at the dawn of morning" (ASV, margin). An incident in the earthly life of our Lord may serve to illustrate this, when He arose and rebuked the wind and said unto the sea, "Peace be still. And the wind ceased, and there was a great calm" (Mk 4:39). Our psalm gives us the antitype of this. "The heathen raged, the kingdoms were moved: he uttered his voice, the earth melted" (Ps 46:6).

The earth, or, land, here represents its inhabitants who have rebelled against the Lord (cf. Ps 2:1-3), and against His people. But when He comes to their defense, and utters His voice, they will melt away just as "all the inhabitants of Canaan" melted away (Ex 15:15) when He brought His people into that land. That same voice will yet make "wars to cease unto the end of the earth (Ps 46:9). Not until then shall we see the end of "wars and rumors of wars"; not by some edict of the United Nations, but by the almighty voice of Him who alone can say, "Be still, and know that I am God: I will be exalted among the heathen [nations], I will be exalted in the earth" (v. 10). It was by His voice that He brought the present creation into being. "He spake, and it was done; he commanded, and it stood fast" (Ps 33:9). The new order of things will come into being in the same way. And the grand purpose of it all will be that He may be exalted in the earth.

To be associated with Him will be a great honor. And that is the force of the refrain in this psalm. "The LORD of hosts is with us; the God of Jacob is our refuge. Selah" (Ps 46:7). The fact that He is here called "the God of Jacob" indicates that this wonderful association is all of grace, whereas His title, "the LORD of hosts," emphasizes His great power. Such a combination is unique; it is divine. It is the culmination of all that is said about Him in verse 1.

The word for *refuge* in verses 7 and 11 is different from that in verse 1. This refuge is more than a place of safety and security, wonderful as that is. This is a high place, or, high fortress, from which one may survey the whole scene and see it as God sees it. Such a philosophy of life is held by those who are citizens of "the city of God." And we who are "a colony of heaven" (Phil 3:20, Moffatt) belong in that category. We who believe in the Lord Jesus are destined to be with Him where He is (Jn 14:3) and to be like Him, for we shall see Him as He is (1 Jn 3:2). "And every man that hath this hope in him purifieth himself, even as he is pure" (1 Jn 3:3). Meanwhile, it is possible for the child of God to live without fear, but not apart from communion with God. We are exhorted "therefore, that, first of all, supplications, prayers, intercessions, and giving of thanks, be made for all men; For kings, and for all that are in authority; that we may lead a quiet and peaceable life in all godliness and honesty" (1 Ti 2:1-2). And we are further exhorted to "be careful for nothing; but in every thing by prayer and supplication with thanksgiving let your requests be made known unto God. And the peace of God, which passeth all understanding, shall keep your hearts and minds through Christ Jesus" (Phil 4: 6-7).

19

PSALM 49

"Like the Beasts That Perish"

THE HUMBLING COMPARISON "like the beasts that perish," occurs twice in Psalm 49. And since the psalm is addressed to all classes and conditions of men, it must have a message for all, even though it has to do mostly with rich men. In this respect, it is quite similar to parts of the books of the Proverbs and Ecclesiastes, as well as the gospel of Luke and the epistle of James in the New Testament.

The problem of wealth and its unequal distribution has occupied the minds of a good many down the ages. But the problem here is concerned with the effects it has upon those who are rich as well as upon those who would like to be rich. It is a common observation that it is not money that is the root of all evil but rather the *love* of it (1 Ti 6:10). And there are comparatively few of whom it can be said that they do not love money. It was when the Israelites were about to enter the promised land that Moses had to warn them saying, "When thy herds and thy flocks multiply, and thy silver and thy gold is multiplied and all that thou hast is multiplied; Then thine heart be lifted up, and thou forget the LORD thy God, which brought thee forth out of the land of Egypt, from the house of bondage . . . And thou shalt say in thine heart, My power and the might of mine hand hath gotten me this wealth" (Deu 8:13-14, 17).

The patriarchs Abraham, Isaac, and Jacob were all rich men. Job must have been a rich man, for he is described as "the greatest of all the men of the east" (Job 1:3). It is not the possession of wealth that is dangerous but the effect it has on the possessor.

Then, too, a rich man—or any man, for that matter—may think

that "money answereth all things" (Ec 10:19). Such was the boast of the church of the Laodiceans to whom the Lord said, "Thou sayest, I am rich, and increased with goods, and have need of nothing; and knowest not that thou art wretched, and miserable, and poor, and blind, and naked" (Rev 3:17). With good reason, many believe that these words apply to the professing church of our day.

It is to such a problem that the psalmist addresses himself with the confidence and authority of one who knows whereof he speaks. "My mouth shall speak of wisdom; and the meditation of my heart shall be of understanding" (Ps 49:3). But he is only the mouthpiece of Another. Disclaiming originality he says, "I will incline mine ear to a parable" (v. 4), or, "the riddle of life," as it has been rendered. He opens his "dark saying upon the harp" to hear the music of his message, even though it be in a minor key.

After an introduction like that, he may well ask the question, "Wherefore should I fear in the days of evil," or adversity, even though that adversity be complicated by the iniquity of his foes who surround him (v. 5, NASB). Right there he puts his finger on one of the evils sometimes practiced by the wealthy. In a similar vein, James asks of those who would favor the rich, "Do not rich men oppress you, and draw you before the judgment seats? Do not they blaspheme that worthy name by the which ye are called?" (Ja 2:6-7).

Money may answer all things "under the sun," but even in that there is one great exception. "They that trust in their wealth, and boast themselves in the multitude of their riches; none of them can by any means redeem his brother, nor give to God a ransom for him." Another translation makes this quite clear. "No man can by any means redeem his brother, Or give to God a ransom for him—For the redemption of his soul is costly, And he should cease trying forever—That he should live on eternally; That he should not see the pit" (Ps 49:7-9, NASB). Even if he should "gain the whole world" that would not suffice (Mt 16:26).

The apostle Peter reminds us that we are "not redeemed with corruptible things, as silver and gold . . . But with the precious blood of Christ, as of a lamb without blemish and without spot" (1 Pe 1:18-19). Even the sacrifices prescribed by the law, having only a shadow of good things to come, can never with those sacrifices which are offered year by year make the comers thereunto perfect, or, complete (Heb 10:1).

> Not all the blood of beasts,
> On Jewish altars slain,
> Could give the guilty conscience peace,
> Or wash away its stain.
>
> But Christ, the heavenly Lamb,
> Took all our guilt away,
> A sacrifice of nobler name,
> And richer blood than they.
>
> ISAAC WATTS

Since "by one man sin entered into the world, and death by sin; and so death passed upon all men, for that all have sinned" (Ro 5:12), it follows that no one could qualify as a redeemer for another. "But God commendeth his love toward us, in that, while we were sinners, Christ died for us" (Ro 5:8).

The possession of material wealth may make a difference in this life, but, "Wise men die, likewise the fool and the brutish person perish, and leave their wealth to others" (Ps 49:10). They cannot take it with them. "Their inward thought is, that their houses shall continue for ever, and their dwelling places to all generations." They even "call their lands after their own names" (v. 11), of which we find an example in Genesis 4:17.

"Nevertheless man being in honour abideth not: he is like the beasts that perish" (v. 12). Destined to "have dominion over the fish of the sea, and over the fowl of the air, and over the cattle, and over all the earth, and over every creeping thing that creepeth upon the earth" (Gen 1:26), he fell to where he is no better than they, so far as this life is concerned. "This their way is their folly: yet their posterity approve their sayings. Selah" (Ps 49:13).

At this point, the psalmist calls for a pause, in order that we may stop and think about that. Are the sayings of the ancients as valid as some think they are? The world has produced some great thinkers, and men love to quote them. The apostle Paul actually quoted one of them when he addressed the Epicureans and Stoics on Mars' hill (Ac 17:28). But even though they claimed to be "the offspring of God," they did not know Him. Their altar "to the unknown god" was evidence of that. In that regard, they were "like the beasts that perish." In their opinion, Paul was nothing more than a "babbler," because he preached unto them "Jesus and the resurrection." To them who perish, the preaching of the cross is foolishness, "but unto us which are saved it is the power of God" (1 Co 1:18).

After another pause, the psalmist describes the funeral of those who "trust in their wealth, and boast themselves in the multitude of their riches" (Ps 49:6). "They are appointed as a flock for Sheol; Death shall be their shepherd: And the upright shall have dominion over them in the morning, and their beauty shall be for Sheol to consume, That there be no habitation for it" (v. 14, ASV).

The mention of "the morning" here implies that there is another day coming. Death does not end all. It is but an intermediate state. As a matter of fact, it is here presented as a shepherd over those who enter Sheol, the abode of the dead, till that morning when all must be manifested before the one to whom all judgment has been committed (Jn 5:22). Associated with Him are those who are referred to in Psalm 49:14 as "the upright." Yes, "The saints shall judge the world" (1 Co 6:2).

The psalmist is careful to distinguish himself from those of whom he has been speaking. Says he, "But God will redeem my soul from the power of the grave [Sheol]; for he shall receive me. Selah" (Ps 49:15). That which no man can do for him, God will do. Not only will He redeem from the grave, or, Sheol, but from the very power of it. In that statement we can see how the psalmist's faith anticipated the day when He who, because "the children are partakers of flesh and blood, he also himself likewise took part of the same; that through death he might destroy him that had the power of death, that is, the devil; And deliver them who through fear of death were all their lifetime subject to bondage" (Heb 2:14-15).

It has been pointed out that when the psalmist said, "He shall receive me" (Ps 49:15), he used the same word which Moses used when he said of Enoch, "He was not; for God took him" (Gen 5:24).

Verse 15 marks a turning point in Psalm 49. Accordingly, we are asked to pause, to stop, and to think about that! Having done that, we need not be afraid when one is made rich, when the glory of his house is increased; "For when he dieth he shall carry noth-

ing away: his glory shall not descend after him" (v. 17). Like the
rich man of whom we read in the New Testament, this rich man
may say to his soul, "Soul, thou hast much goods laid up for many
years; take thine ease, eat, drink, and be merry. But God said
unto him, Thou fool, this night thy soul shall be required of thee:
then whose shall those things be which thou hast provided?" (Lk
12:19-20). His future is grim indeed. "He shall go to the generation of his fathers; they shall never see the light" (Ps 49:19).

The fact that he goes to the generation of his fathers distinguishes
him from the beast. The beast has no future, but man does. "Who
knoweth the spirit of man that goeth upward, and the spirit of the
beast that goeth downward to the earth?" (Ec 3:21). "It is appointed unto men once to die, but after this the judgment" (Heb
9:27).

Man may be like the beast in his death, but there the similarity
ends. It is the "after this" that makes the difference. This is graph-
ically portrayed in the story of the rich man and Lazarus. When
the latter died, he "was carried by the angels into Abraham's
bosom: the rich man also died, and was buried; And in hell [Hades]
he lift up his eyes, being in torments, and seeth Abraham afar off,
and Lazarus in his bosom. And he cried and said, Father Abraham, have mercy on me, and send Lazarus, that he may dip the
tip of his finger in water, and cool my tongue; for I am tormented
in this flame. But Abraham said, Son, remember that thou in thy
lifetime receivedest thy good things, and likewise Lazarus evil things:
but now he is comforted and thou art tormented. And beside all
this, between us and you there is a great gulf fixed: so that they
which would pass from hence to you cannot; neither can they pass
to us, that would come from thence" (Lk 16:22-26). The tables
are turned, and the rich man reaps as he had sowed.

James also warns the rich man saying, "Go to now, ye rich men,
weep and howl for your miseries that shall come upon you. Your
riches are corrupted, and your garments are motheaten. Your gold
and silver is cankered; and the rust of them shall be a witness
against you, and shall eat your flesh as it were fire. Ye have heaped
treasure together for the last days. Behold, the hire of the labour-
ers who have reaped down your fields, which is of you kept back
by fraud, crieth: and the cries of them which have reaped are entered into the ears of the Lord of sabaoth. Ye have lived in pleasure

on the earth, and been wanton; ye have nourished your hearts, as in a day of slaughter" (Ja 5:1-5). These solemn words require no comment, except to say that even in our day there are laborers working in the great harvest field who are neglected by their wealthier brethren. The selfish ones will be the losers in that day when every one shall "receive the things done in his body, according to that he hath done, whether it be good or bad" (2 Co 5:10). But our psalmist is dealing with those who "shall never see the light."

In this wealthy nation of ours, there are many who can say, "Soul, thou hast much goods laid up for many years; take thine ease, eat, drink, and be merry" (Lk 12:19). Such will discover when it is too late that the soul does not live on material things. "Is not the life more than meat, and the body than raiment? (Mt 6:25).

"The blessing of the LORD, it maketh rich, and he addeth no sorrow with it" (Pr 10:22).

20

PSALM 51

A Broken and a Contrite Heart

THIS PENITENTIAL PSALM is remarkable because it does not contain one word of excuse for the sins committed. Neither is there any attempt on the part of the sinner to tone down the gravity of his offences or to blame others for what he has done. The fault is all his own: "my transgression," "mine iniquity," and "my sins." These things had their roots in a sinful nature communicated to him when his mother conceived him. But when he says, "In sin did my mother conceive me" (Ps 51:5), he means that, like all of us since the fall, *she* was not in a state of innocence but "in sin," or "outside of Paradise," as another has put it.

The one who said to our first parents, "Be fruitful, and multiply" (Gen 1:28), was not telling them to do something sinful. He created them "male and female" for that very purpose. And, "marriage is honourable in all, and the bed undefiled" (Heb 13:4). God cannot be blamed for what man has done to that sacred relationship.

The plea for mercy with which Psalm 51 begins shows that the speaker does not blame God for the plight which he is in. In his helplessness, he casts himself upon the mercy and the lovingkindness of God who only can blot out his transgressions by washing him thoroughly from his iniquity and cleansing him from his sin. Without pleading extenuating circumstances, or using situation ethics, he acknowledges his transgressions, and confesses his sin.

Even though the particular sin in view here was against Uriah the Hittite, in measuring the enormity of his crime, the psalmist goes to the highest level, God Himself. "Against thee, thee only, have I sinned, and done this evil in thy sight" (v. 4). This is not without parallel in Scripture. The prodigal had certainly sinned against his father, but when he made his confession, he said, "Father, I have sinned against heaven, and in thy sight, and am no more worthy to be called thy son" (Lk 15:21), using language very similar to that of the psalmist. In like manner, Paul wrote, "All have sinned, and come short of the glory of God" (Ro 3:23).

If the gravity of an offence is measured by the dignity of the person offended, and it is, then the sin of the psalmist is grave indeed. And here it may be said that the greater includes the less. That David had sinned against Uriah as well, goes without saying. But God had said long before that "whoso sheddeth man's blood, by man shall his blood be shed: for in the image of God made he man" (Gen 9:6). Therefore murder is primarily a sin against God. And David justifies God in that. It was only through God's mercy and lovingkindness that he escaped the death penalty.

But the work of restoration must go deeper than forgiveness. God desires "truth in the inward parts." And the psalmist is in full accord with that for he says, "In the hidden part thou shalt make me to know wisdom" (Ps 51:6). It would be sad indeed if the awful experience which occasioned this psalm did not make him wiser. "The fear of the Lord is the beginning of wisdom: and the knowledge of the holy is understanding" (Pr 9:10). And that will lead quite naturally to a desire for cleanliness. "Purge me with hyssop, and I shall be clean: wash me, and I shall be whiter than snow" (Ps 51:7). Hyssop was used on three occasions in the Old Testament: for the sprinkling of the blood of the passover lamb (Ex 12:22), in the cleansing of a leper (Lev 14:1-7), and for the sprinkling of the "water of separation" as "a purification for sin" (Num 19:9). No doubt it is to this last that the psalmist refers here.

The discipline necessary to bring him to repentance is likened to the breaking of his bones, a painful process to be sure. "Now no chastening for the present seemeth to be joyous, but grievous: nevertheless afterward it yieldeth the peaceable fruit of righteousness unto them which are exercised thereby" (Heb 12:11). The result is that he is made to "hear joy and gladness" (Ps 51:8).

In addition to cleansing, the psalmist prays that the record of his sins may be blotted out as well. Then, realizing that out of the heart "are the issues of life," he prays that God would create in him a clean heart, and renew a right spirit within him (v. 10). In this he anticipates, seemingly, the New Testament doctrine, "If any man be in Christ, he is a new creature: old things are passed away; behold, all things are become new" (2 Co 5:17).

In verse 11 he speaks as one who has the Holy Spirit. In his "last words" he claimed that the Spirit of the LORD spoke by him (2 Sa 23:1-2). As an Old Testament prophet, "the Spirit of Christ" was in him (1 Pe 1:11). In view of the fact that the Holy Spirit convicts of sin, righteousness, and judgment (Jn 16: 8-11), his prayer—"Take not thy holy spirit from me" (Ps 51: 11)— is very remarkable. This shows a "right spirit" indeed (v. 10).

Memories of happier days move him to pray, "Restore unto me the joy of thy salvation; And uphold me with a willing spirit" (v. 12, ASV).

It is interesting to observe that right after he mentions the Holy Spirit, he prays that the joy of God's salvation may be restored to him. Joy is a fruit of the Spirit (Gal 5:22). It has often been noticed that he did not pray for the restoration of salvation, but for the joy of it. Having confessed his sins, the way would be clear for God to do just that. "If we confess our sins, he is faithful and just to forgive us our sins, and to cleanse us from all unrighteousness" (1 Jn 1:9).

Forgiveness and cleansing go together. This is stressed repeatedly in this psalm. "Wash me thoroughly from mine iniquity, and cleanse me from my sin" (v. 2). "Purge me with hyssop, and I shall be clean: wash me, and I shall be whiter than snow" (v. 7). "Hide thy face from my sins, and blot out all mine iniquities" (v. 9). "Deliver me from bloodguiltiness, O God, thou God of my salvation: and my tongue shall sing aloud of thy righteousness" (v. 14).

The mention of bloodguiltiness marks the depth to which one may go in his sin against God and man. "At every point at which we touch His creatures, we touch God Himself; every blow struck at them is struck at Him. . . . The guilt of every sin is fundamentally the same, revolt against God: this is, in a true sense, the only sin."* In view of this we may well marvel at the readiness with which those who demanded the crucifixion of Christ could say, "His

*F. W. Grant, *The Numerical Bible*, vol. 3, *The Psalms*, p. 203.

blood be on us, and on our children" (Mt 27:25), thus incriminating themselves and their posterity as well.

The psalmist is quite the opposite of them. As one cleansed and restored, he is ready now to teach transgressors God's ways so that sinners may be converted unto Him (Ps 51:13). Delivered from bloodguiltiness, he says, "My tongue shall sing aloud of thy righteousness. O Lord, open thou my lips; and my mouth shall shew forth thy praise" (vv. 14-15). Even though there were no animal sacrifices provided for the sins which he had committed, he could bring the sacrifice of "a broken spirit: a broken and a contrite heart" (v. 17). Such sacrifices God will not despise. They are "acceptable to God by Jesus Christ" (1 Pe 2:5). "By him therefore let us offer the sacrifice of praise to God continually, that is, the fruit of our lips giving thanks to his name" (Heb 13:15).

The closing verses of Psalm 51—supposedly added by another— speak of God being "pleased with the sacrifices of righteousness, with burnt-offering and whole burnt-offering" (v. 19). According to the eighteenth verse, these will be offered when God in His good pleasure unto Zion builds again the walls of Jerusalem. That, I take it, will be in the millennium and that "these are the ordinances of the altar in the day when they shall make it, to offer burnt-offerings thereon, and to sprinkle blood thereon" (Eze 43:18). In Old Testament times, such sacrifices pointed forward to Christ; in the millennium, they will look back to Him and His cross, as memorials, in remembrance of Him.

> O mystery of mysteries!
> Of life and death the tree;
> Centre of two eternities,
> Which look, with rapt, adoring eyes,
> Onward and back to Thee—
> O Cross of Christ, where all His pain
> And death is our eternal gain.
>
> J. G. DECK

21

PSALM 56

"Put Thou My Tears into Thy Bottle"

ALMOST IMMEDIATELY after Adam and Eve had sinned, the LORD God said to Eve, "I will greatly multiply thy sorrow and thy conception; in sorrow shalt thou bring forth children." And to Adam He said, "Cursed is the ground for thy sake; in sorrow shalt thou eat of it all the days of thy life" (Gen 4:16, 17). And so the history of man began with sorrow upon sorrow.

Sorrow and tears usually go together. The Bible mentions practically all of the patriarchs weeping at one time or another. Job said, "My friends scorn me: but mine eye poureth out tears unto God" (Job 16:20). For an entirely different reason, "Abraham came to mourn for Sarah, and to weep for her" (Gen 23:2). Of Joseph it is recorded that he wept tears of sorrow as well as tears of joy. David was a great weeper, and so was Jeremiah. In the New Testament, Paul said, "I have great heaviness and continual sorrow in my heart . . . for my brethren, my kinsmen according to the flesh" (Ro 9:2-3). Peter "wept bitterly" after denying his Lord (Mt 26:75). John also "wept much, because no man was found worthy to open and to read the book, neither to look thereon" (Rev 5:4). The shortest verse in the Bible tells us that "Jesus wept" (Jn 11:35). And we are of like passions, men as well as women.

Of course, all do not weep for the same reason. In Psalm 42:3, the psalmist says that his tears have been his meat day and night because of those who taunt him saying, "Where is thy God?" In the psalm now before us, he weeps because "Mine enemies would daily swallow me up" (Ps 56:2). Their daily fighting against him oppressed him. According to one commentator, they were panting after him like wild beasts, thirsting for his blood.

100

Peter used similar words when describing our adversary the devil, walking about as a roaring lion, "seeking whom he may devour" (1 Pe 5:8). But in so doing, he adopts various methods.

The psalmist says, "Every day they wrest my words: all their thoughts are against me for evil. They gather themselves together, they hide themselves, they mark my steps, when they wait for my soul" (Ps 56:5-6). By twisting something the psalmist may have said, or by quoting it out of context, they "wrest" his words. This, of course, is common practice, especially among those who hate the children of God. They are quick to take advantage of any ambiguity to make one say the exact opposite of what he actually said.

Then too the wicked mark our steps and are quick to point out any inconsistency in our walk and behavior. That is why we are exhorted, "Walk circumspectly, not as fools, but as wise, Redeeming the time, because the days are evil" (Eph 5:15-16). Fear is another thing which the enemy uses quite frequently to "swallow up" God's people.

But the psalmist knew the cure for that. "What time I am afraid, I will trust in thee. In God will I praise his word, in God I have put my trust; I will not fear what flesh can do unto me" (Ps 56:3-4). And again in verse 11, he says, "In God have I put my trust: I will not be afraid what man can do unto me."

It should be noted that the psalmist repeatedly links praise with his faith, and that in turn is linked with the Word of God. (See vv. 4 and 10.) Not a few have witnessed to the fact that a song of praise to God delivered them from all fear. Of that we have a classic example in the New Testament. In the darkness of the inner prison, with their feet fast in the stocks, "At midnight Paul and Silas prayed, and sang praises unto God; and the prisoners heard them. And suddenly there was a great earthquake, so that the foundations of the prison were shaken: and immediately all the doors were opened, and every one's bands were loosed" (Ac 16:24-26). They prayed—that was faith; and they sang—that was praise. And thus they were delivered from anything that "flesh" might do to them.

While it is true that "we wrestle not against flesh and blood" (Eph 6:12), the enemy does use "flesh" at times to accomplish his ends. To Eve, he came in the form of a serpent; to Joseph and David, in the form of beautiful women; and to our blessed Lord, in Judas Iscariot. And he has many accomplices. "They be many that fight against me" (Ps 56:2). They may differ otherwise but in their hatred of God's child, they are united. "They gather themselves together, they hide themselves" (v. 6). They like to work undercover. Even Satan himself sometimes operates as "an angel of light" (2 Co 11:14).

But they shall not "escape by iniquity" (Ps 56:7). God is not indifferent, nor unmoved by that which His servant is enduring at the hands of the enemy. He "tells" or, counts, the wanderings of His people, and puts their tears in His bottle. There is a play on words here. The word for *wanderings* and the word for *bottle* are very similar in the original. Bottles used in Bible times were usually made of the skin of some clean animal, such as the sheep or goat, and they contained water, milk, or other liquids. The use of the word here is poetic, of course, but highly suggestive of the many tears the psalmist had shed. But the Lord takes note of every tear. The day is coming when He will wipe each tear from our eyes (Rev 7:17). In that day "He will wipe away tears from off all faces; and the rebuke of his people shall he take away from off all the earth: for the LORD hath spoken it" (Is 25:8). Then, "There shall be no more death, neither sorrow, nor crying, neither shall there be any more pain: for the former things are passed away" (Rev 21:4).

> Not now, but in the coming years—
>   It may be in the better land—
> We'll read the meaning of our tears,
>   And there, some time, we'll understand.
>
> God knows the way, He holds the key,
>   He guides us with unerring hand;
> Some time with tearless eyes we'll see;
>   Yes, there, up there, we'll understand.
>
> M. N. CORNELIUS

Even in his day the psalmist could say, "God is for me" (Ps 56:9), thus anticipating the apostle who wrote, "If God be for us, who can be against us?" (Ro 8:31). The psalmist was not only taking God at His word, he was praising Him for it. And that led to courage: "I will not be afraid what man can do unto me" (Ps 56:11).

As evidence of his gratitude he says, "Thy vows are upon me, O God: I will render praises unto thee" (v. 12) or, "I will render thank offerings to thee" (NASB). One form of the thank offering was a "vow, or a voluntary offering" (Lev 7:16). The psalmist would make such an offering, because the Lord had delivered his soul from death.

Surely every Christian can say as much. And because He has delivered our souls from death, let us present, as a thank offering, our "bodies a living sacrifice, holy, acceptable unto God" (Ro 12:1). In so doing, we may be sure that He will deliver our feet from falling, so that we may walk before Him in the light of the living.

"When Abram was ninety years old and nine, the LORD appeared to Abram, and said unto him, I am the Almighty God; walk before me, and be thou perfect [or, sincere]" (Gen 17:1). To walk "in the light of the living" (Ps 56:13) is to "walk in the light, as he is in the light" (1 Jn 1:7). "But the path of the just is as the shining light, that shineth more and more unto the perfect day" (Pr 4:18). And "There shall be no night there" (Rev 22:5), because the perfect day has no end.

22

PSALM 57

The Shadow of Thy Wings

In the opening chapter of his second letter to the Corinthians, Paul presents God as "the Father of mercies, and the God of all comfort," or, encouragement. The concept was not a new one. It occurs here and there in the Old Testament, particularly in the Psalms. It is implied in such expressions as "the shadow of thy wings," poetic to be sure, but very heartwarming. Boaz used it when speaking to Ruth the Moabitess, saying, "The Lord recompense thy work, and a full reward be given thee of the Lord God of Israel, under whose wings thou art come to trust" (Ru 2:12).

It is because of the excellence of God's loving-kindness that the children of men put their trust under the shadow of His wings (Ps 36:7). One commentator has observed that no such concept occurs in heathen literature. Our Lord used it in His lament over Jerusalem. "O Jerusalem, Jerusalem, thou that killest the prophets, and stonest them which are sent unto thee, how often would I have gathered thy children together, even as a hen gathereth her chickens under her wings, and ye would not" (Mt 23:37).

In this psalm, 57, David speaks of the shadow of God's wings as a place of refuge until certain calamities be "overpast." As long as we are in this world, they will never be "overpast" (Jn 16:33). But this place of refuge will be available until we reach that place where the wicked cease from troubling and the weary are at rest (Job 3:17).

"He shall send from heaven, and save me from the reproach of him that would swallow me up. Selah. God shall send forth his mercy and his truth" (Ps 57:3). In so doing, He may employ angels who are "ministering spirits, sent forth to minister for them who shall be heirs of salvation" (Heb 1:14). Perhaps we have become too sophisticated to believe that. But there it is in God's Word, which also furnishes us with examples of how He does this.

The psalmist likens his position to that of one whose "soul is among lions: and I lie even among them that are set on fire, even the sons of men, whose teeth are spears and arrows, and their tongue a sharp sword." When Daniel was among literal lions, God sent His angel and "shut the lions' mouths" (Dan 6:22) that they should not hurt him. When Herod had imprisoned Peter, intending to kill him as he did James the brother of John, the Lord sent His angel and delivered him "out of the hand of Herod, and from all the expectation of the people of the Jews" (Ac 12:11). Even our blessed Lord was the object of angelic ministry when He was surrounded by "lions" (Lk 22:43).

David's enemies also prepared a net for his steps, under which was a pit they had dug to catch him. But "in vain the net is spread in the sight of any bird" (Pr 1:17). In all of these experiences, David was learning what God will do for those who trust in Him. Yes, God was performing all things for him (Ps 57:2). To perform means to finish or complete something. God does not do things by halves. It is written of Abraham that "he staggered not at the promise of God through unbelief; but was strong in faith, giving glory to God; And being fully persuaded that, what he had promised, he was able also to perform (Ro 4:20-21). Paul also assures us that "he which hath begun a good work in you will perform it until the day of Jesus Christ" (Phil 1:6).

All of this should be an encouragement to any of the Lord's servants who may be harrassed by the evil one and his emissaries. "Fear not: for they that be with us are more than they that be with them" (2 Ki 6:16). Let us be childlike enough to believe it. The same one who stood by Paul in his time of need (Ac 23:11) will stand by us. And, "Greater is he that is in you, than he that is in the world" (1 Jn 4:4).

Our enemies may prepare a net for our steps and dig a pit before us, but the Lord can turn them back and even make them fall into the very pit they have prepared for us. Because of this, we may say with the psalmist, "My heart is fixed, O God, my heart is fixed: I will sing and give praise" (Ps 57:7). A fixed heart is a heart that has found its true resting place in the shadow of His wings. In spiritual matters, the heart is more important than the head. It was with the hearts of His own disciples that the Lord Jesus was concerned just before He went to the cross. Said He, "Let not your heart be troubled, neither let it be afraid" (Jn 14: 27). He wanted their hearts to be fixed.

A fixed heart will be a singing heart. "At midnight Paul and Silas prayed, and sang praises unto God: and the prisoners heard them. And suddenly there was a great earthquake, so that the foundations of the prison were shaken: and immediately all the doors were opened, and every one's bands were loosed" (Ac 16:25-26). "He brought them out of darkness and the shadow of death, and broke their bands in sunder" (Ps 107:14).

In like manner David, when he fled from Saul in the cave, could say, "Awake up, my glory [or, soul, RSV]; awake, psaltery and harp: I myself will awake early. I will praise thee, O Lord, among the people: I will sing unto thee among the nations" (Ps 57:8-9). His praise increases in volume and extent as he calls upon psaltery and harp to accompany it. It is a time of triumph and victory! "For thy mercy is great unto the heavens, and thy truth unto the clouds" (v. 10).

This is the second time that God's mercy, or loving-kindness, and His truth are mentioned in this psalm. "All the paths of the LORD are mercy and truth unto such as keep his covenant and his testimonies" (Ps 25:10). In Him alone, "Mercy and truth are met together; righteousness and peace have kissed each other" (Ps 85: 10). In saying that God's loving-kindness reaches unto the heavens and His truth unto the clouds, the psalmist is telling us that God is "able to do exceeding abundantly above all that we ask or think" (Eph 3:20). These things originate in heaven, but it is on earth that they are displayed in all of their fullness and perfection.

In the refrain which occurs in verses 5 and 11 of Psalm 57, the psalmist rises to great heights in his worship of the Lord. "Be thou exalted, O God, above the heavens: let thy glory be above all the earth." The answer to this may be seen in the prayer of the apostle Paul who prayed that we might know what is the exceeding greatness of God's power "to us-ward who believe." It is this power "which he wrought in Christ, when he raised him from the dead, and set him at his own right hand in the heavenly places, Far above all principality, and power, and might, and dominion, and every name that is named, not only in this world, but also in that which is to come" (Eph 1:19, 20-21).

But none of this isolates Him from His own. "For thus saith the high and lofty One that inhabiteth eternity, whose name is Holy; I dwell in the high and holy place, with him also that is of a contrite and humble spirit, to revive the spirit of the humble, and to revive the heart of the contrite ones" (Is 57:15). Such is the blessed experience of those who take refuge under the shadow of His wings.

> Under His wings I am safely abiding;
> Though the night deepens and tempests are wild,
> Still I can trust Him; I know He will keep me;
> He has redeemed me, and I am His child.
>
> > Under His wings, under His wings,
> > Who from His love can sever?
> > Under His wings my soul shall abide,
> > Safely abide forever.
>
> Under His wings, what a refuge in sorrow!
> How the heart yearningly turns to His rest!
> Often when earth has no balm for my healing,
> There I find comfort, and there I am blest.
>
> Under His wings, O what precious enjoyment!
> There will I hide till life's trials are o'er;
> Sheltered, protected, no evil can harm me;
> Resting in Jesus, I'm safe evermore.
>
> WILLIAM O. CUSHING

23

PSALM 63

Thirsting for God

To be in the place of God's choosing and yet not to be satisfied, sounds peculiar. But such was the situation of the psalmist as he thirsted for God in a dry and thirsty land. According to Joshua 15, "the wilderness of Judah" (where David wrote Psalm 63) was that part of the land of Canaan which was assigned to the tribe of Judah by lot. In those days that was the divinely established way of determining who got what. "The lot is cast into the lap; but the whole disposing thereof is of the LORD" (Pr 16:33). David belonged to the tribe of Judah; therefore this was God's choice for him.

The divine purpose in choosing such a portion for him may be inferred from the opening verses of the psalm. It was to teach him that only God can satisfy the deepest cravings of the human heart. Had he been assigned a situation where "every prospect pleases," he might never have learned that. Modern examples of this may be found in any congregation of God's people. A physician, dying of an incurable disease, was asked what, if anything, he had learned through his illness. His reply, "I learned to know God." A similar question was asked of a helpless cripple, and she replied, "I have learned to look up." The psalmist not only learned to know God as his own God, but that He could be found by those who seek Him. He is not far from every one of us (Ac 17:27). He is "a very present help in trouble" (Ps 46:1).

But there is a time to seek Him. The psalmist said, "Early will I seek thee" (Ps 63:1), not only in the early hours of the day, but before we seek anything or anyone else. How often we seek Him only as a last resort. Or, as some have put it, "When you can't do

108

anything else, you can pray." True enough, but why do last that which should have been first?

The psalmist had a twofold longing for God. "My *soul* thirsteth for thee, my *flesh* longeth for thee" (v. 1). In other words,' he longed for God with his whole being. The thirst and the longing are synonymous. Together they constitute the utmost of intense desire. Like most of us, David had probably sought satisfaction elsewhere before he turned to God. In so doing he would discover that very often that which promises satisfaction turns out to be nothing but a "dry and thirsty land, where no water is" (v. 1).

In verse 2 David defines for us what he really longed for. He wanted to see God's power and His glory out there in "the wilderness of Judah," as he had seen Him "in the sanctuary" (v. 2). He would know God not only as the one who dwells "in the high and holy place" but "with him also that is of a contrite and humble spirit, to revive the spirit of the humble, and to revive the heart of the contrite ones" (Is 57:15).

But God's power and His glory go together. When the sisters of Lazarus sent unto the Lord saying, "Lord, behold, he whom thou lovest is sick" (Jn 11:3), He replied, "This sickness is not unto death, but for the glory of God, that the Son of God might be glorified thereby" (Jn 11:4). He did not hasten to the bedside of Lazarus but "abode two days still in the same place where he was" (Jn 11:6). Meanwhile, Lazarus died. When the Lord announced his death, He added, "And I am glad for your sakes that I was not there, to the intent ye may believe" (Jn 11:15). Then, just before calling Lazarus back to life, He gently rebuked Martha, saying, "Said I not unto thee, that, if thou wouldest believe, thou shouldest see the glory of God?" (Jn 11:40). The exercise of His power had its counterpart in the glory of God. All will agree that the resurrection of Lazarus was far more glorious than the healing of his sickness could have been.

Apparently the psalmist was aware of the divine balance between God's power and His glory. By faith he had looked behind the scenes to see God "in the sanctuary." Things look entirely different from that point of view. When Asaph went into the sanctuary, then he understood (Ps 73:17). We too may "enter into the holiest by the blood of Jesus" (Heb 10:19), to see and understand as they

did. It was there that David discovered that God's loving-kindness
is better than life.

And the result is that complaint gives place to worship. "My
lips shall praise thee. Thus will I bless thee while I live: I will lift
up my hands in thy name" (Ps 63:3-4). His thirst was quenched
and his soul revived. It has been noted that being "filled with
the Spirit" is followed immediately by, "Speaking to yourselves in
psalms and hymns and spiritual songs, singing and making melody
in your heart to the Lord" (Eph 5:18, 19).

Because of such fullness, the psalmist could say, "My soul shall
be [or, is] satisfied as with marrow and fatness," words which sig-
nify richness and abundance. This is another example of blessing
"exceeding abundantly above all that we ask or think." Because
of this, he says, "My mouth shall praise thee with joyful lips" (Ps
63:5) which is easy enough when all is going well and we are
surrounded by many others who are praising the Lord. It is another
matter when one is all alone, especially in "the night watches," with
their attendant weariness and longing for the dawn. But very often
these are times when memory functions undisturbed, and meditation focuses our thoughts on Him who was our help when other
helpers failed and comforts fled. Then, because Has been our
help, we can say with the psalmist, "Therefore in the shadow of thy
wings will I rejoice" (v. 7).

But we have not yet reached the end of the way. And, as always,
the home stretch demands our utmost. A successful finish will de-
pend on how closely we follow the Lord. As Paul neared the end,
he could honestly say, "I have fought a good fight, I have finished
my course, I have kept the faith" (2 Ti 4:7). Paul is an outstanding
example of what it means to follow hard after the Lord.

The way by which He leads is an upward way, where progress
depends on fresh spiritual impulses at every step. Very often, because we do not take the time for spiritual refreshment, we lag behind and lose direct contact with the Lord. No doubt it was to pre-
vent this that Barnabas, when he came to Antioch, "exhorted them
all, that with purpose of heart they would cleave unto the Lord"
(Ac 11:23). It was when "Peter followed him afar off" (Mt 26:
58) that he not only lost touch with the Lord, but weakened to the
point where he denied Him. Notice how the psalmist connects two

things here: "My soul followeth"; "Thy right hand upholdeth," and in that order (Ps 63:8).

The upward way is beset by foes whose avowed purpose is to destroy us. The apostle describes them for us as wicked spirits· in high places (Eph 6:12). To ward them off, we need "the whole armour of God" (Eph 6:13), which includes "the sword of the Spirit, which is the word of God" (Eph 6:17). Our psalmist tells us that our enemies "shall fall by the sword: they shall be a portion for foxes" (Ps 63:10). There is something ironic about this last expression. If he had said "a portion for lions" that would have been in keeping with the professed might of the enemy. "A portion for foxes" implies that they were not so strong after all.

In direct contrast we are introduced to one who is truly mighty. "The king shall rejoice in God" (v. 11). Unseen until now, He appears as He did in Joshua's day, as the "captain of the host of the LORD" (Jos 5:14), rejoicing in God, and leading His own in triumph (2 Co 2:14) from "victory unto victory." He will not disappoint those who trust in Him. "Every one that sweareth by him shall glory: but the mouth of them that speak lies shall be stopped" (Ps 63:11). Shouts of acclamation on the one hand, dead silence on the other!

In the presence of the King, the thirst for God is completely satisfied. "And he that sitteth on the throne shall dwell among them. They shall hunger no more, neither thirst any more; neither shall the sun light on them, nor any heat. For the Lamb which is in the midst of the throne shall feed them, and shall lead them unto living fountains of waters: and God shall wipe away all tears from their eyes" (Rev 7:15-17).

"And the Spirit and the bride say, Come. And let him that heareth say, Come. And let him that is athirst come. And whosoever will, let him take the water of life freely" (Rev 22:17).

24

PSALM 73

"Until . . . Nevertheless"

A GOOD DEAL depends on one's point of view. Even facts may appear to differ, depending on the point of view and the point of time from which they are observed. Like the psalmist Asaph, we may be fully persuaded of the goodness of God and yet have questions concerning apparent contradictions to it. This can be so disturbing that we find ourselves slipping where we should be standing firm. We may even sink so low that we become "envious at the foolish" when we see the prosperity of the wicked. Everything seems to go well with them, even in the hour of death. "Their strength is firm. They are not in trouble as other men; neither are they plagued like other men" (Ps 73:4b-5). But appearances are sometimes deceiving.

"Therefore pride compasseth them about as a chain," or, a necklace, and "violence covereth them as a garment" (v. 6). This combination dates back to the days of Noah. "There were giants in the earth in those days . . . mighty men which were of old, men of renown" (Gen 6:4). But, "The earth also was corrupt before God, and the earth was filled with violence" (Gen 6:11). The psalmist found himself in another age of affluence. "Their eyes stand out with fatness: they have more than heart could wish" (Ps 73:7), or, "They exceed the imaginations of their heart." And our Lord Jesus has warned us that history will repeat itself (Lk 17:26-30). The conditions in the end times will again be like the days of Noah.

One of the evidences of man's depravity is his ingratitude. "When they knew God, they glorified him not as God, neither were thankful" (Ro 1:21). Instead, "They set their mouth against the heavens" (Ps 73:9), which is but another way of saying that they speak

112

against God. The ultimate of this will be seen in the beast to whom was given "a mouth speaking great things and blasphemies. . . . And he opened his mouth in blasphemy against God, to blaspheme his name. . . . And it was given unto him to make war with the saints, and to overcome them" (Rev 13:5-7).

Since God is in heaven and beyond their reach, the wicked persecute His people to the point where they wonder if God really knows what is going on. In days yet to come, those who will be slain for the Word of God and for the testimony which they hold, will cry out, saying, "How long, O Lord, holy and true, dost thou not judge and avenge our blood on them that dwell on the earth?" (Rev 6:10). Meanwhile their persecutors "prosper in the world; they increase in riches" (Ps 73:12). Despising the riches of God's "goodness and forbearance and longsuffering," the wicked ignore the very thing which would lead them to repentance and blessing. According to their hardness and impenitent heart, they treasure up unto themselves wrath against the day of wrath and revelation of the righteous judgment of God, who will render to every man according to his deeds (Ro 2:4-6).

With his eyes still on these sinners in their present prosperity, the psalmist concludes that he has cleansed his heart and his hands in vain. What's the use? But on second thought, he realizes that to talk like that might stumble some other child of God, "For none of us liveth unto himself" (Ro 14:7). Better not to say what one has been thinking than to cause a weaker brother to stumble (cf. Ro 14:13). After all, there might be a solution to his problem. And there was!

The time had come to take another look at things from a different viewpoint. It was when Asaph went into the sanctuary of God that he understood. To a man of the world, this might look impractical. Mundane things must be dealt with on a worldly level. But for the child of God, this is the most practical thing that ever was. To go into the sanctuary of God is to go into the holy presence of Him before whose eyes "all things are naked and opened" (Heb 4:13). To see things from His point of view is to see them in their proper perspective. What looked so firm from the lower level now appears to be "slippery places" (Ps 73:18). Those who walk there are doomed to destruction and desolation, and to be "utterly consumed with terrors" (v. 19).

When He whom they thought to be asleep awakes He will "despise their image" (v. 20). Many are concerned about their "image" these days. How disconcerting to find it despised by Him who is not deceived by a superficial appearance! "The LORD seeth not as man seeth; for man looketh on the outward appearance, but the LORD looketh on the heart" (1 Sa 16:7). The effect of all this was tremendous. "My heart was grieved, and I was pricked in my reins. So foolish was I, and ignorant: I was as a beast before thee" (Ps 73:21-22). To be in the sanctuary of God and to see things from His viewpoint is both edifying and humbling. But, "He that humbleth himself shall be exalted" (Lk 14:11).

What that exaltation consists of is seen in the closing verses of this psalm. "Nevertheless I am continually with thee: thou hast holden me by my right hand" (Ps 73:23). All of us like to believe that the Lord is with us. We claim it every time we repeat the Twenty-third Psalm. But to say to the Lord, "I am continually with thee" implies that I am in full fellowship with all He says and does. However good my intentions, I could never do this in my own strength. But He is ready to hold my right hand. And, "Because he is at my right hand, I shall not be moved" (Ps 16:8). In the very place where Satan would stand to accuse (Zec 3:1), there the Lord comes to our defense. Realizing this, the psalmist can say with confidence, "Thou shalt guide me with thy counsel, and afterward receive me to glory" (Ps 73:24), an intimation of the glorious prospect that is before us.

All of this leads quite naturally to a deep appreciation of the one who makes all this possible. "Whom have I in heaven but thee? and there is none upon earth that I desire beside thee" (v. 25). These words find their ultimate expression in Christ whom God hath highly exalted and "given him a name which is above every name" (Phil 2:9). This is the one who is not only the strength of our heart, but our "portion for ever" (Ps 73:26). Eternal satisfaction!

Not all will share in this. Those that are far from God, by their own choice, shall perish. These are the ones who "set their mouth against the heavens" (v. 9). But there are those who can say with the psalmist, "It is good for me to draw near to God: I have put my trust in the Lord GOD" (v. 28). They too were far off, but are now made nigh by the blood of Christ (Eph 2:13). And their great objective is that they may declare all His works.

> When all Thy mercies, O my God,
>   My rising soul surveys,
> Transported with the view, I'm lost
>   In wonder, love, and praise.
>
> Through ev'ry period of my life
>   Thy goodness I'll pursue;
> The desert past, in glory bright,
>   The precious theme renew.
>
> Through all eternity to Thee
>   A joyful song I'll raise;
> But oh, eternity's too short
>   To utter all Thy praise.
>
> JOSEPH ADDISON

25

PSALM 80
"The Bread of Tears"

EXCEPT FOR THE BOOKS of Jeremiah and Lamentations, the psalms have more to say about tears than any other book in the Bible. In Psalm 80, the psalmist speaks of "the bread of tears" (v. 5). A similar expression occurs in Psalm 42:3, "My tears have been my meat day and night," another way of saying, "Instead of eating, I have wept." In like manner it is said of Hannah, the mother of Samuel, that "she wept, and did not eat" (1 Sa 1:7).

It was the "Shepherd of Israel" (Ps 80:1) who fed His people with "the bread of tears" and gave them "tears to drink in great measure" (v. 5). His people were as "sheep going astray." But here we see them crying out to Him as "the Shepherd and Bishop" of their souls (1 Pe 2:25). They speak of Him as leading Joseph like a flock, and yet as the one who dwells between the cherubim. It was there that He promised to meet with Moses and commune with him "from above the mercy seat, from between the two cherubims which are upon the ark of the testimony" (Ex 25:22).

In their march through the wilderness, this occupied the central place in the procession. The tribes of Ephraim, Benjamin, and Manasseh, mentioned in Psalm 80:2, constituted "the third rank" in that procession, immediately following the "tabernacle of the congregation . . . in the midst of the camp" (Num 2:17-24). From this we gather that they maintained the divinely prescribed order, even though they were not following their Guide. They had order, but they did not have the light of His countenance.

When the LORD led His people out of Egypt, He went before them in a pillar of cloud by day, and a pillar of fire by night (Ex 13:22). If they had faithfully followed Him, there would have

116

been no need to pray, "Turn us again, O God, and cause thy face to shine; and we shall be saved" (Ps 80:3).

It was in answer to that prayer that He fed them with the bread of tears. This is still an Eastern figure of speech for affliction. But the Lord "doth not afflict willingly nor grieve the children of men" (Lam 3:33). His purpose in making them eat the bread of tears was to bring them to repentance. That it had the desired effect is seen in Psalm 80, verses 3, 7, and 19, where we hear them pray, "Turn us again, O God, and cause thy face to shine," and each time with greater intensity. This is a prayer for restoration uttered by those who, because of their deviation, had become a strife to their neighbors and a laughingstock among their enemies (v. 6).

Worse than either of these things was the fact that the Lord was "angry against the prayer" of His people (v. 4). What that prayer was, we are not told. We may be quite sure that it was not the thrice-repeated prayer we have already noticed. That was one prayer He would be waiting to hear. It may be that they prayed for a change of diet. The bread of tears is not very pleasant food. Had they been in the right state of soul, "He should have fed them also with the finest of the wheat: and with honey out of the rock" would He have satisfied them (Ps 81:16).

While the prodigal son was in the far country, "he would fain have filled his belly with the husks that the swine did eat," the bread of tears for him (Lk 15:16). But when he turned in repentance to his father, he was feasted at the banqueting table instead. Of this our psalm says nothing. But, "The Lord is merciful and gracious, slow to anger, and plenteous in mercy. He will not always chide: neither will he keep his anger for ever. He hath not dealt with us after our sins; nor rewarded us according to our iniquities" (Ps 103:8-10).

In the second part of this psalm, we see the Lord in a different role. Here He is no longer appealed to as the Shepherd of Israel, but as the Husbandman who "brought a vine out of Egypt" and "cast out the heathen, and planted it" (Ps 80:8). Nothing is said about the wilderness journey, such as we saw in verses 1 and 2. The whole book of Joshua is summed up in nine words: "Thou hast cast out the heathen, and planted it" (v. 8, only three words in the original). In its new location, the vine prospered so that "the hills were covered with the shadow of it, and the boughs thereof were like the goodly cedars. She sent out her boughs unto the sea, and her branches unto the river" (vv. 10-11); the western and eastern boundaries of the land as promised to Joshua (Jos 1:4).

Much is said about the boughs and branches, but the principal thing for which a vine exists is not even mentioned. There is no mention made of fruit. The Lord "looked that it should bring forth grapes, and it brought forth wild grapes . . . For the vineyard of the LORD of hosts is the house of Israel, and the men of Judah his pleasant plant: and he looked for judgment, but behold oppression; for righteousness, but behold a cry" (Is 5:2b, 7). What a disappointment! Could it be that He is saying the same thing of the church? Our Lord spoke of Himself as the true vine and His Father as the Husbandman. And we are the branches in that vine, from whom He has a right to expect fruit. Said He, "Herein is my Father glorified, that ye bear much fruit; so shall ye be my disciples" (Jn 15:8).

When He did not get the fruit He desired, He broke down the hedges of the vine, "so that all they which pass by the way might pluck her. The boar out of the wood doth waste it, and the wild beast of the field doth devour it" (Ps 80:12-13). Thus the psalmist describes the powers which took God's people captive, devastated their land, and destroyed their temple. And, "All these things happened unto them for ensamples [types]; and they are written for our admonition" (1 Co 10:11). The lessons to be learned are timeless and exactly suited to our own times. What happened to Israel in those days has its antitype in what is happening in the church today. We need to pray as the psalmist did, "Look down from heaven, and behold, and visit this vine; And the vineyard which thy right hand hath planted, and the branch that thou madest strong for thyself" (Ps 80:14-15).

The transition here from the boughs and branches (plural) to the branch (singular) is interesting (cf. vv. 11, 15). It is well known that in the Old Testament our Lord is referred to a number of times as "the Branch." That He is the Branch whom the Lord made strong for Himself is confirmed in verse 17: "Let thy hand be upon the man of thy right hand, upon the son of man whom thou madest strong for thyself." I believe we have here a direct reference to the Messiah, our Lord Jesus Christ, who often referred to Himself as the "Son of man." And He it is who is at the right hand of God, making intercession for us (Ro 8:34). In that sacred place, He exercises a twofold ministry as Priest and Advocate. On the one hand, He prays that our faith may not fail (Lk 22:32)˙ for "he ever liveth to make intercession" for us (Heb 7:25). On the other hand, as our Advocate, He pleads our cause when in our folly and weakness, we have sinned against Him. Because of this we can pray, as does the psalmist, "Stir up thy strength, and come and save us" (Ps 80:2). And again, "Turn us again, O LORD God of hosts, cause thy face to shine; and we shall be saved" (v. 19).

"So will not we go back from thee" (v. 18) is a promise that only He can enable us to keep. "Quicken [revive] us, and we will call upon thy name" (v. 18). That we need revival, individually and collectively, is acknowledged by all who are concerned about the spiritual state of the church today. In spite of the fact that we see some encouragement in the evangelistic crusades which have been so greatly blest of God, we have yet to see a genuine revival. Many churches are actually recording a decrease in membership. Even if the reverse were the case, mere expansion is not a sign of life, as we have seen.

In addition to the lack of fruit is the absence of that radiancy that should mark us as the children of God. That this was felt by the psalmist is evidenced by the fact that three times he prayed, "Cause thy face to shine; and we shall be saved" (v. 19). Since God is light, His face never ceases to shine. It is our faces that cease to shine because we have not been looking at His.

It was not for a change of diet that they prayed, but for the shining of His face. This is followed by the assurance, "And we shall be saved" (v. 19). It has been pointed out that the word *salvation* has three tenses. There is a sense in which we, as believers in the Lord Jesus, become saved (Ro 10:9). Then there is a sense in which salvation is still future (Ro 5:9). But in between these two there is what may be called the present tense of salvation. Right now we "are kept by the power of God through faith unto salvation" (1 Pe 1:5). It is in this last sense that the word *saved* is used in our psalm. Our being saved is spoken of here as the direct result of the shining of His face, and this is the shining that we are to reflect. "They looked unto him, and were lightened [radiant]: and their faces were not ashamed" (Ps 34:5). In so doing we shall be saved from falling and its resultant misery.

I recall a picture I saw some years ago in a Chicago newspaper. It was a picture of commuters leaving the Northwestern railway depot on their way to the Loop. The caption: "The Thrombosis Brigade." So far as I could tell, there was not one radiant face in the crowd. Undoubtedly, there were many Christians among them. But the radiance which is the result of a quiet time with the Lord, if they had had it, was no longer visible. The news in the paper that morning, plus the cares of the day ahead, were probably enough to dim their light to the point of extinction. That which should have distinguished them as having been with Jesus was no longer there.

"Turn us again, O LORD God of hosts, cause thy face to shine; and we shall be saved." Amen.

26

PSALM 90

"All Our Days"

PSALM 90 was written by a man who probably never knew what it is like to have a fixed home (cf. Ex 2:22). He found his true home in the one who is God "from everlasting to everlasting," and in whose sight a thousand years "are but as yesterday when it is past, and as a watch in the night" (Ps 90:4). Peter may have had this verse in mind when he wrote, "But, beloved, be not ignorant of this one thing, that one day is with the Lord as a thousand years, and a thousand years as one day. The Lord is not slack concerning his promise, as some men count slackness; but is longsuffering to us-ward, not willing that any should perish, but that all should come to repentance" (2 Pe 3:8-9).

Psalm 90:6 mentions morning and evening. From that point on to the end of the psalm, the emphasis is on "our days" and "our years."

The psalm is probably the oldest in the whole collection. It was written by "Moses the man of God" who lived till he was 120 years old with his vision unimpaired and his natural force unabated (Deu 34:7). Two more of his psalms, or songs, are recorded in Deuteronomy 32 and 33. It is quite generally believed that he wrote this psalm near the close of Israel's journey through the wilderness, and shortly before he entered into the presence of the Lord. Therefore it should be of special interest to any who, like him, are nearing the end of their earthly pilgrimage.

The psalm begins with the sovereignty of God. The Hebrew word for *Lord* implies that. This is linked immediately with the fact that He has "been our dwelling place in all generations" (Ps 90:1). Such a combination is very striking. Of course, it was for

Israel that he was making this claim. But I see no reason why we may not claim it also. Our Lord said, "If any man love me, he will keep my words: and my Father will love him, and we will come unto him, and make our abode with him" (Jn 14:32). "Hereby know we that we dwell in him, and he in us, because he hath given us of his Spirit" (1 Jn 4:13). Would to God we were more aware of it!

It is the Lord in whom "we live, and move, and have our being" (Ac 17:28). And He is the one who has the authority to say, "Return ye children of men" (Ps 90:3), "for dust thou art, and unto dust shalt thou return" (Gen 3:19). But there is that in us which was not made of dust, "the breath of life," which was breathed into man's nostrils, "and man became a living soul" (Gen 2:7). We have a treasure in these earthen vessels which is imperishable. And, "Though our outward man perish, yet the inward man is renewed day by day" (2 Co 4:16).

In His discipline (Ps 90:7-11) He may even destroy the flesh "that the spirit may be saved in the day of the Lord Jesus" (1 Co 5:5). "For whom the Lord loveth he chasteneth, and scourgeth every son whom he receiveth. If ye endure chastening, God dealeth with you as with sons; for what son is he whom the father chasteneth not?" (Heb 12:6-7).

"Now no chastening for the present seemeth to be joyous, but grievous: nevertheless afterward it yieldeth the peaceable fruit of righteousness unto them which are exercised thereby" (Heb 12:11). All of this is to "teach us to number our days, that we may apply our hearts unto wisdom" (Ps 90:12). Some years ago, I began to number my days with this verse in mind. Having passed the fourscore mark and then some, I feel the need more than ever, to apply my heart unto wisdom, "redeeming the time, because the days are evil." We may be busy but not wise. "Wherefore be ye not unwise, but understanding what the will of the Lord is" (Eph 5:16, 17).

"The days of our years are threescore years and ten; and if by reason of strength they be fourscore years, yet is their strength labour and sorrow; for it is soon cut off, and we fly away" (Ps 90:10). These words are suggestive. In the case of an individual like Lazarus the beggar, they might mean to be "carried by the angels into Abraham's bosom" (Lk 16:22). But for those of us who may "remain unto the coming of the Lord" (1 Th 4:15), they could mean to be "caught up together with them in the clouds, to meet the Lord in the air; and so shall we ever be with the Lord" (1 Th 4:15). In that case we can see how appropriate it would be to pray, "Return, O LORD, how long?" (Ps 95:13; cf. Rev 22:20). In our psalm, however, it is a prayer for the resumption of His favor which was interrupted by their iniquities and their secret sins (v. 8). But, "If we confess our sins, he is faithful and just to forgive us our sins, and to cleanse us from all unrighteousness" (1 Jn 1:9). In that sense He repents concerning His servants (Ps 90:13).

The beautiful prayer that follows this plea is one I love to pray. "O satisfy us early with thy mercy; that we may rejoice and be glad all our days" (v. 14). "For he that will love life, and see good days, let him refrain his tongue from evil, and his lips that they speak no guile: Let him eschew evil, and do good; let him seek peace, and ensue it" (1 Pe 3:10-11).

According to verse 15 of Psalm 90, there is a correspondence between past sorrow and future joy; between chastisement and the peaceable fruit thereof. "Make us glad *according* to the days wherein we have seen evil." Such a request is in keeping with the Lord's way of dealing with His own, for "He hath not dealt with us after [or, according to] our sins; nor rewarded us according to our iniquities" (Ps 103:10).

At this point the psalmist turns from all that he and his people had done, to what the Lord has done. "Let thy work appear unto thy servants, and thy glory unto their children" (Ps 90:16). The failures of God's servants often have a very sad effect on their children. But if they can be made to see the work of God in our lives, not only in saving us but in restoring us after we have wandered from Him, they may profit by our experience. And to give unto us "beauty for ashes, the oil of joy for mourning, the garment of praise for the spirit of heaviness; that we may be called trees of righteousness, the planting of the LORD, that he might be glorified" (Is 61:3). In any event, "We know that, when he shall appear, we shall be like him; for we shall see him as he is. And every man that hath this hope in him purifieth himself, even as he is pure" (1 Jn 3:2-3).

Finally, we have a reference to "the work of our hands," that it too may be established upon us (Ps 90:17). Of that we get a beautiful example in the New Testament, where we are called upon to " 'rejoice and be glad and give the glory to Him, for the marriage of the Lamb has come, and His bride has made herself ready.' And it was granted her to clothe herself in fine linen, bright and clean; for the fine linen is the righteous acts of the saints" (Rev 19:7-8, NASB). Thus what she has done will be established upon her. It is for this purpose that we must all appear, or be manifested, before "the judgment seat of Christ; that every one may receive the things done in his body, according to that he hath done, whether it be good or bad" (2 Co 5:10). "Therefore judge nothing before the time, until the Lord come, who both will bring to light the hidden things of darkness, and will make manifest the counsels of the hearts: and then shall every man have praise of God" (1 Co 4:5). Until then, as it was said to Asher, "Thy shoes shall be iron and brass; and as thy days, so shall thy strength be" (Deu 33:25).

27

PSALM 114

Obstacles Overcome

IF EVER there was a nation that had obstacles to overcome, it was the nation of Israel. But in the overcoming of those obstacles, they set a pattern for God's people, no matter what their historical period may be. The things which happened to them serve as types, or, examples, and they are written for our learning and encouragement (Ro 15:4; 1 Co 10:11).

Because of their long residence in Egypt, there would naturally be a tendency to resist any radical change, unless it were for the better. It would not be easy after all those years to pull up stakes and leave behind their friends and familiar surroundings, as well as the relative security against invasion by an enemy nation. Then too, the journey across the wilderness of Sinai was not very inviting. And the land which was to be their future home was inhabited by nations who were sure to resist their entrance.

All of these things suggest a number of reasons why the Israelites would be reluctant to leave Egypt in spite of the fact that they were slaves there. Not long after they left Egypt they said, "Would to God we had died by the hand of the LORD in the land of Egypt, when we sat by the flesh pots, and when we did eat bread to the full" (Ex 16:3). And yet, according to this psalm, they "went out of Egypt." It does not say that they were forced out, nor even that they were led out. We may be sure that no Egyptian news reporter would describe the exodus in that way. They left Egypt of their own accord!

The description of Egypt given here is interesting. That which is called "the house of bondage" elsewhere in the Bible, as well as "the iron furnace" (Deu 4:20), is here described as "a people of a

strange language" (Ps 114:1). When we take into account the fact
that the Israelites had lived in Egypt for a long time, this is quite
remarkable. In our own country a first-generation American would
hardly refer to English as a strange language. Israel had lived in
Egypt long enough to know the language of that country as well
if not better than their own Hebrew.

But "the children of this age" have ways of expressing themselves which are indeed "a strange language" to the redeemed of
the Lord. Profanity, obscenity, and even the slang so common today, should be a "strange language" to us. The same may well have
been the case in the days of Moses. Christians are exhorted to use
"sound speech, that cannot be condemned; that he that is of the
contrary part may be ashamed, having no evil thing to say of you"
(Titus 2:8); "For by thy words thou shalt be justified, and by thy
words thou shalt be condemned" (Mt 12:37).

In contrast to the "people of a strange language," we are told
that when "the house of Jacob" went out of Egypt "Judah was his
sanctuary, and Israel his dominion" (Ps 114:2). I take it that the
pronoun *his* refers to the LORD, even though He has not yet been
named in this psalm. That being so, this means that He had made
this people His sacred dwelling place, His sanctuary, as well as
"His dominion," the place where He was acknowledged as sovereign. "His sanctuary" suggests priesthood and "His dominion" the
place where He reigns. Thus two things are brought together which
may also be seen in the royal priesthood of Melchisedec, of which
our Lord is the great High Priest (Heb 4:14). And, "Such an high
priest became us, who is holy, harmless, undefiled, separate from
sinners, and made higher than the heavens" (Heb 7:26). To have
Him dwell among us and to rule over us, is a privilege indeed!

Although God is sovereign, it appears from Psalm 114:3 that
certain evil powers tried to contest His complete control. "The sea
saw it, and fled: Jordan was driven back." The fact that the sea
and the Jordan are personified here suggests that they are symbolic
of powers that would hinder, or impede, if possible, the exodus of
God's people as they left Egypt and all that it represents.

The Red Sea is here joined with the Jordan as if they were two
parts of the same thing. So far as Israel's experience was concerned,
they were separated by forty years. Of the one it is said that it fled,
and of the other that it was driven back (Ps 114:3). Satan was

counting on either the sea or the pursuing Egyptian army to destroy the Israelites. Instead, the sea which might have swallowed up the Israelites was made to serve as "a wall unto them on their right hand, and on their left. Thus the LORD saved Israel that day out of the hand of the Egyptians; and Israel saw the Egyptians dead upon the sea shore" (Ex 14:29-30). The Lord not only foiled Satan's plan in that one instance, in the New Testament we learn that a part of His ministry was "to preach deliverance to the captives, and . . . to set at liberty them that are bruised" (Lk 4:18). He took the part of flesh and blood "that through death he might destroy him that had the power of death, that is, the devil; And deliver them who through fear of death were all their lifetime subject to bondage" (Heb 2:14-15).

It could be that Israel's deliverance from Egypt illustrates this New Testament spiritual truth. We do know that when the exodus was in progress, "The LORD looked unto the host of the Egyptians through the pillar of fire and of the cloud, and troubled the host of the Egyptians, And took off their chariot wheels, that they drave them heavily: so that the Egyptians said, Let us flee from the face of Israel; for the LORD fighteth for them against the Egyptians" (Ex 14:24-25). This, I believe, is what the sea witnessed and caused it to flee.

In His presence even mountains are made to skip "like rams and the little hills like lambs" (Ps 114:4). A spiritual interpretation of this may be seen in the words of our Lord. "Verily I say unto you, If ye have faith as a grain of mustard seed, ye shall say unto this mountain, Remove hence to yonder place; and it shall remove; and nothing shall be impossible unto you. Howbeit this kind goeth not out but by prayer and fasting" (Mt 17:20-21). The biographies of men and women of faith abound in examples of how the Lord removes the mountains and hills of difficulty in answer to believing prayer. And I am old-fashioned enough to include the fasting.

There is a note of sarcasm in the apostrophe which follows in Psalm 114:5-6. "What ailed thee, O thou sea, that thou fleddest? thou Jordan, that thou wast driven back? Ye mountains, that ye skipped like rams; and ye little hills, like lambs?" This is not unlike the apostle Paul who wrote, "O death, where is thy sting? O grave, where is thy victory?" (1 Co 15:55). It was not because

of Israel, however, but because of "the presence of the Lord, at
the presence of the God of Jacob" (Ps 114:7) that the waters fled
and the mountains moved, as He opened up the way before them.
Nor is it because of us that He works similar miracles today. "But
thanks be to God, which giveth us the victory through our Lord
Jesus Christ" (1 Co 15:57). He is "the Lord," sovereign in His
might, and "the God of Jacob," just as sovereign in His grace.

What He did to the Red Sea and to the Jordan He did once for
all. But to supply the people of Israel with water during the forty
years in between these events required further miracles. To meet
that need, God "turned the rock into a standing water, the flint into
a fountain of waters." To implement this, the Lord said to Moses,
"Behold, I will stand before thee there upon the rock in Horeb;
and thou shalt smite the rock, and there shall come water out of it,
that the people may drink. And Moses did so in the sight of the
elders of Israel" (Ex 17:6). This striking of the rock, so manifest-
ly typical of what was done to our blessed Lord on the cross, was
never to be repeated. He who was smitten there needs not to suffer
again and again. "This man, after he had offered one sacrifice for
sins for ever, sat down on the right hand of God" (Heb 10:12).
But the same one who told His servant Moses to strike the rock,
spoke to him again, saying, "Take the rod, and gather thou the
assembly together, thou, and Aaron thy brother, and speak ye unto
the rock before their eyes; and it shall give forth his water, and
thou shalt bring forth to them water out of the rock: so shalt thou
give the congregation and their beasts drink" (Num 20:8). Because they disobeyed God, neither Moses nor Aaron was permitted
to bring the congregation into the land (Num 20:12). But God did
not fail His people on their account, even though Moses smote the
rock twice. "The water came out abundantly, and the congregation
drank, and their beasts also" (Num 20:11). In addition to this,
they "did all drink the same spiritual drink: for they drank of that
spiritual Rock that followed them: and that Rock was Christ"
(1 Co 10:4). Thus did God overcome the greatest obstacle of
all, their unbelief, that they "might be filled with all the fulness of
God" (Eph 3:19).

> When Israel by divine command,
> The pathless desert trod,

death, of which we get a glimpse in the case of a rich man who "died, and was buried; And in hell [hades] he lift up his eyes, being in torments, and seeth Abraham afar off, and Lazarus in his bosom. And he cried and said, Father Abraham, have mercy on me, and send Lazarus, that he may dip the tip of his finger in water, and cool my tongue; for I am tormented in this flame" (Lk 16:22b-24). These are solemn words which God has used many times with man, "To bring back his soul from the pit, to be enlightened with the light of the living" (Job 33:30).

The psalmist took these things to heart. Then he called upon the name of the Lord to deliver his soul, and the Lord heard him. "Gracious is the LORD, and righteous; yea, our God is merciful" (Ps 116:5). In that sentence we may see all of the elements of "the gospel of Christ: [which] is the power of God unto salvation to every one that believeth; to the Jew first, and also to the Greek. For therein is the righteousness of God revealed from faith to faith" (Ro 1:16-17). It is here that "mercy and truth are met together; righteousness and peace have kissed each other" (Ps 85:10). Such a plan of redemption is absolutely unique; it is divine. Well may we exclaim, "Who is a God like unto thee, that pardoneth iniquity? . . . because he delighteth in mercy (Mic 7:18).

All that is required on our part is to be simple enough to believe and to receive it. "The LORD preserveth the simple: I was brought low, and he helped me," or, saved me (Ps 116:6). Like the blind man whose eyes the Lord opened (Jn 9), the psalmist may not have known the how of it, but of one thing he was sure: the Lord had saved him. And knowing that, he could say to his soul, "Return unto thy rest, O my soul; for the LORD hath dealt bountifully with thee" (Ps 116:7). The Lord had filled him "with all joy and peace in believing" (Ro 15:13).

The Lord's bountiful dealing with him consisted of three things. "Thou hast delivered my soul from death, mine eyes from tears, and my feet from falling." The death sentence—"The soul that sinneth, it shall die" (Eze 18:4)—was borne by Him "who knew no sin," that we might become God's righteousness in Him (2 Co 5:21). The sacrifices offered in Old Testament times were types of Christ's death. Our Lord fulfilled them all when He died for us on the cross and "gave himself a ransom for all, to be testified in due time" (1 Ti 2:6). Therefore those who hear His word and believe on Him are "passed from death unto life" (Jn 5:24). Their souls are delivered from death.

The eyes which once wept tears of regret and repentance are now made to look with unblurred vision to Him who will one day wipe every tear from our eyes (Rev 21:4). He will forever remove the cause of tears and thus deliver our eyes from tears.

And the feet which in time past "walked according to the course of this world" (Eph 2:2) now gladly tread "the path of the just" which is as "the shining light, that shineth more and more unto the perfect day" (Pr 4:18). The psalmist wanted to "walk before the LORD in the land of the living" (Ps 116:9), even as He walked (1 Jn 2:6). Thus his feet are delivered from falling.

In the second part of the psalm, beginning at verse 10, we see what it means to "walk before the LORD." It is a walk of faith, "For we walk by faith, not by sight "(2 Co 5:7), or as the psalmist says, "I believed, therefore have I spoken." His was a very simple creed. He not only knew what he believed, but whom. In that he reminds us of Paul who said, "I know whom I have believed, and am persuaded that he is able to keep that which I have committed unto him against that day" (2 Ti 1:12). Truly, "The LORD preserveth the simple" (Ps 116:6).

In his letter to the Corinthians, Paul had this passage in mind when he wrote, "We having the same spirit of faith, according as it is written, I believed, and therefore have I spoken; we also believe, and therefore speak; Knowing that he which raised up the Lord Jesus shall raise up us also by Jesus, and shall present us with you" (2 Co 4:13-14). The addition here, as well as the application, are very interesting and instructive. The apostle, by the Holy Spirit, makes explicit that which was implicit in the psalmist's simple creed.

Apparently the psalmist had sought help from men only to discover that he could not rely on any of them. All of their proffered solutions to his problem proved false. As a result, he "was greatly afflicted," or, greatly perturbed so that he said in his haste, "All men are liars" (Ps 116:11). Not a few have made similar statements after a great disappointment. The psalmist was very human.

After that statement of extreme pessimism, the psalmist turns to brighter themes. The Lord had blessed him with innumerable benefits, so that he exclaimed, "What shall I render unto the LORD for all his benefits toward me?" (v. 12). The Christian believer may well ask the same question, because he has been blessed "with all spiritual blessings in heavenly places in Christ" (Eph 1:3).

At first sight, the response to this rhetorical question may sound strange. But Psalm 116:13 might be rendered, "I will lift up the cup of salvation," as if he were offering this cup to the Lord as a drink offering. The drink offering was usually offered with some other offering, such as "a burnt-offering, or a sacrifice in performing a vow, or in a freewill-offering" (Num 15:3). It is symbolic of joy.

The apostle Paul, in writing to the Philippians, spoke of his service for the Lord in this way. Said he, "If I be poured out as a drink-offering upon the sacrifice of your faith, I joy, and rejoice with you all" (Phil 2:17, KJV margin). And in his last letter, as he faced martyrdom, he wrote, "I am already being poured out, and the time of my release is come" (2 Ti 4:6, Greek).

In the same spirit, as it were, the psalmist says, "I will pay my vows unto the LORD now in the presence of all his people" (Ps 116:14). Should that involve the laying down of his life for the Lord's sake, the psalmist is content to know that "precious in the sight of the LORD is the death of his saints" (v. 15). For that he would claim no special honor. After all, he was but a servant and the son of a servant.

Paradoxical as it may sound, he is also the Lord's freeman. "Thou hast loosed all my bonds" (v. 16). In these few words, he sums up all that the Lord had done for him. In heartfelt appreciation, he says, "I will offer to thee the sacrifice of thanksgiving, and will call upon the name of the LORD" (v. 17). The thank offering, like "a vow, or a voluntary offering," was actually a peace offering (Lev 7:11-16). The peace offering is symbolic of communion, because part of it was offered to the Lord, and part of it was eaten by the offerer. In it we may see gratitude, devotion, and worship. It is on this chord that the psalm closes.

The application of these things to us as Christians is just as becoming as it was to the psalmist. By our Lord Jesus, let us also "offer the sacrifice of praise to God continually, that is, the fruit of our lips giving thanks to his name. But to do good and to communicate forget not: for with such sacrifices God is well pleased" (Heb 13:15-16). "Praise ye the LORD" (Ps 116:19). Or, as it is in the original, "Hallelujah!"

29

PSALM 120

"In My Distress I Cried"

APART FROM THE LAST CLAUSE in verse 1, there is not a glad note in the whole of Psalm 120. While it is true that the psalmist is probably speaking of some hateful foe, such as Doeg the Edomite, it is also possible to see here the description of an inner conflict such as Paul gives us in Romans 7.

The source of the psalmist's trouble is a common one. In James 3 we find another expression of the same problem. Who of us is there who has not regretted at some time that he did not speak "the truth, the whole truth, and nothing but the truth"? Of course we try to excuse ourselves by saying that exaggeration and hyperbole are not actually deceit. But a tender conscience does not always let us get away with that, even though kind friends, realizing their own weaknesses, generously excuse our overstatements. We console ourselves by saying that, after all, there was no "malicious intent to deceive" and that nobody was harmed by our "slight inaccuracies." But when some child or unsuspecting person takes our statements at face value, we realize that less than true statements may be harmful after all.

The fact that the psalmist was distressed by this is a good sign. In his distress, he turned to the one who knew his every thought, word, and deed. And he was heard. God always listens to an honest soul. And we dare not be less than honest in His presence. Accordingly he does not begin with some ambiguity in an attempt to tone down his offence. Neither does he plead extenuating circumstances. Very frankly, the psalmist says, "Deliver my soul, O LORD, from lying lips, and from a deceitful tongue" (Ps 120:2). Without pausing for an answer except to say that he had been heard, he turns now to his tongue in an apostrophe. "What shall be given

134

unto thee? or what shall be done unto thee, thou false tongue?" (v. 3). The law under which the psalmist lived said, "Thou shalt not bear false witness against thy neighbour" (Ex 20:16). The New Testament more positively says, "Wherefore putting away lying, speak every man truth with his neighbour: for we are members one of another" (Eph 4:25).

"The tongue is a little member, and boasteth great things. Behold, how great a matter a little fire kindleth! And the tongue is a fire, a world of iniquity: so is the tongue among our members, that it defileth the whole body, and setteth on fire the whole course of nature; and it is set on fire of hell [or, gehenna]" (Ja 3:5-6). This is the consequence of the unrefrained use of the false tongue. "Sharp arrows of the mighty, with coals of juniper" (Ps 120:4). A terrible harvest!

"The tongue can no man tame; it is an unruly evil, full of deadly poison. Therewith bless we God, even the Father; and therewith curse we men, which are made after the similitude of God" (Ja 3:8-9). But, "The LORD shall cut off all flattering lips, and the tongue that speaketh proud things" (Ps 12:3).

The psalmist's environment did not help any. It made matters worse. "Woe is me, that I sojourn in Mesech, that I dwell in the tents of Kedar" (Ps 120:5). From among these neighbors, he singles out one who hates peace. This is the one who is elsewhere described as "that old serpent, called the Devil, and Satan, which deceiveth the whole world" (Rev 12:9). He not only makes war on the saints, but incites others to do so also (Rev 12:17; 13:7). We who live in the world of which he is the prince know what it means to dwell "with him that hateth peace" (Ps 120:6). But the God of peace will bruise him under our feet shortly (Ro 16:20). Until then let us use our tongues to preach "peace by Jesus Christ" (Ac 10:36), who could truly say, "I am for peace." He is not only for peace, He is peace personified. And the day is coming when every tongue shall confess that He is Lord, to the glory of God the Father (Phil 2:11).

> O for a thousand tongues to sing
> My great Redeemer's praise,
> The glories of my God and King,
> The triumphs of His grace.

My gracious Master and my God,
  Assist me to proclaim,
To spread through all the earth abroad,
  The honors of Thy name.

CHARLES WESLEY

30

PSALM 126

Sowing in Tears

IN THE HISTORY of nations, as in the case of individuals, there are certain times which stand out as extraordinary and unforgettable. In the case of Israel, the exodus would be such an event. But subsequent to that, they experienced something which was equally remarkable—their return from captivity in Babylon. It was so wonderful that it seemed like a dream and not a reality. But when they realized that they were actually free, their mouth was filled with laughter, and their tongue with singing (Ps 126:2). Even the heathen nations recognized this as a divine intervention on their behalf. They said among themselves, "The LORD hath done great things for them" (v. 2).

Such was the case with the Thessalonians in the early days of the church. The news of their conversion to the living and true God spread abroad so that apostles did not need to speak anything. "For they themselves shew of us what manner of entering in we had unto you, and how ye turned to God from idols to serve the living and true God; And to wait for his Son from heaven, whom he raised from the dead, even Jesus, which delivered us from the wrath to come" (1 Th 1:9-10).

But it is one thing to have the mouth filled with laughter and the tongue with singing, and quite another to have the heart filled to overflowing with the joy of the Lord. Evidently the laughter and the singing did not last long. Right after they said, "The LORD hath done great things for us; whereof we are glad" (Ps 126:3), we hear them praying, "Turn again our captivity, O LORD, as the streams in the south" (v. 4). If things are presented in chronological sequence here, then this must refer to some experience

137

comparable to the captivity in Babylon. Spiritually they were right back to where they were before.

And that is a very common experience. Again and again, the Lord delivers us from things that enslave us. And yet, we slip back into them quite easily. In the case of some professed children of God, backsliding has become almost a way of life. But it is always a hopeful sign when there is a desire for revival, as expressed in their prayer, "Turn again our captivity, O LORD, as the streams in the south" (v. 4).

"The streams in the south" were dry a good part of the year. Their flow depended on seasonal rains and the melting of snow and ice in the mountains. In that regard, their "times of refreshing" would be quite typical of the intermittent seasons of blessing in the lives of so many of us. It need not be so, because the Lord has invited us saying, "If any man thirst, let him come unto me and drink. He that believeth on me, as the scripture hath said, from within him shall flow rivers of living water. But this spake he of the Spirit, which they that believed on him were to receive" (Jn 7:37-39, ASV).

When we run dry in spite of this gracious offer, the Lord is not only ready to answer our prayer for revival, but to do exceeding abundantly above all that we ask or think. This He does by beginning a new work, so beautifully depicted in the sowing of seed for a new crop. When the vine brought forth only wild grapes (Is 5), and the fig tree yielded no fruit (Lk 13:6-9), He sent forth the plowman, John the Baptist, to prepare the soil before He went forth to sow (Mt 13:3).

But it was a sowing in tears. The first sowing yielded nothing. The hard ground—the human heart—did not receive the seed, and the birds of the air came and devoured the seed. The second sowing was not much better, but there were some signs of life. But because there was no depth of earth, there was no fruit. The third sowing gave greater promise, but affluence spoiled that by choking the seed. What tears all of this must have cost the Sower!

If there is a lesson to be learned from this, it is that the present material affluence of the church is not a blessing but quite the opposite. The church at Laodicea is quoted as saying, "I am rich, and increased with goods, and have need of nothing," not knowing that it was actually wretched, miserable, poor, blind, and naked

(Rev 3:17). Those five words speak volumes. We have but to think of their opposites to see what that church was missing.

But, thank God, the sowing does not end in failure. The seed sown on good ground "are they, which in an honest and good heart, having heard the word, keep it, and bring forth fruit with patience" (Lk 8:15). And so he that sows in tears reaps in joy. Not deterred by the difficulties and disappointments, "He that goeth forth and weepeth, bearing precious seed [or, seed for scattering] shall doubtless come again with rejoicing, bringing his sheaves with him" (Ps 126:6).

If we think of the Sower here as our Lord Jesus, for He so described Himself in the parable of the Sower (Mt 13:37), then we may trace a striking parallel to what we have in this psalm. He spoke to the men of His generation in parables, "Because they seeing see not; and hearing they hear not, neither do they understand" (Mt 13:13). Because of that, He wept over them, saying, "If thou hadst known, even thou, at least in this thy day, the things which belong unto thy peace! but now they are hid from thine eyes" (Lk 19:42). How often would He have gathered their children together, even as a hen gathereth her chickens under her wings, but they would not! (Mt 23:37).

If He was to come again with rejoicing, bringing His sheaves with Him, He must make a fresh beginning. And that He did when He came to sow the seed for a fresh crop. And the day seems not far off when He will return, bringing His sheaves with Him. "For if we believe that Jesus died and rose again, even so them also which sleep in Jesus will God bring with him" (1 Th 4:14). "For it became him, for whom are all things, and by whom are all things, in bringing many sons unto glory, to make the captain of their salvation perfect through sufferings" (Heb 2:10). He that wept "shall doubtless come again with rejoicing, bringing his sheaves with him."

But He will not be alone in His joy. Psalm 126:5 shows that others also sow in tears, like the Master Himself. They too shall reap in joy. "Lift up your eyes and look on the fields; for they are white already to harvest. And he that reapeth receiveth wages, and gathereth fruit unto life eternal; that both he that soweth and he that reapeth may rejoice together" (Jn 4:35-36).

31

PSALM 130

"Out of the Depths"

WHEN ANYTHING EXCEEDS the limits of our measuring instruments, we generally refer to it as immeasurable or unfathomable. Such were probably the thoughts of the psalmist as he described his situation when he cried unto the Lord in his distress. He does not attempt to tell us how deep those depths were. But in Psalm 130:3, he leaves us in no doubt as to what they were. To quote a well-known hymn, he "was sinking deep in sin." And that may be said not only of a sinner who has never trusted the Saviour but also of a child of God who may have deviated from the way of truth, or, to put it bluntly, who has backslidden. The latter is the case here. Like many another, he may have tried to extricate himself from those depths only to discover that, for him, it was a hopeless task. He would know better, of course than to appeal to any of his fellows. His case was too desperate for that. There was only one who could really help him.

But that one was the very one against whom he had sinned. If He were to mark iniquities, who should stand? (v. 3). That question is a tacit confession of guilt. And the solemn fact is that God does mark iniquities (Rev 20:12). And iniquities are not just little mistakes, or "psychological abnormalities," to quote one professor. They are acts of rebellion against God. And in using the word *iniquities*, the psalmist makes no attempt to minimize his faults. Evidently the law of Moses made no provision for these, whatever they were. If so, he would need only to bring his offering and the priest would make an atonement for him as touching his sin that he has sinned, and it would be forgiven him (Lev 5:13). Since no mention is made here of any offering for sin, I assume that his offence was one for which the law made no provision.

Nevertheless, there was forgiveness with the Lord. The case of David is evidence of that, as may be seen in Psalm 51. David acknowledged his sin unto God; he did not hide his iniquity. He confessed his transgressions unto the Lord, and He forgave the iniquity of David's sin (Ps 32:5). But in forgiving, God is "faithful and just" (1 Jn 1:9), because another "was wounded for our transgressions, he was bruised for our iniquities: the chastisement of our peace was upon him; and with his stripes we are healed. All we like sheep have gone astray; we have turned every one to his own way; and the LORD hath laid on him the iniquity of us all" (Is 53:5-6). Yes, there is forgiveness with Him, that He may be feared (Ps 130:4).

The fact that He has so graciously and so righteously forgiven us should not make us careless or presumptuous. Far from it! Rather, we should be more careful than ever lest in any thing we might grieve Him (Eph 4:30).

Those who have been so graciously cleared of every charge of guilt may now look forward with joy to seeing Him. This was the psalmist's hope. "I wait for the LORD, my soul doth wait, and in his word do I hope" (Ps 130:5). Of course, the psalmist did not wait for the Lord in the same way that we do now. But his language fits our case perfectly. When he says, "My soul doth wait, and in his word do I hope," he lets us know that this hope is something more than a creedal statement which he might repeat without much feeling, as so many do. One can never substitute correct doctrine for a correct relationship with Christ, and extensive knowledge of prophecy will never replace the loving desire to see Him face to face.

In the case of the psalmist, that missing "something" was present in full force. "My soul waiteth for the Lord more than they that watch for the morning: I say, more than they that watch for the morning" (v. 6). He was not waiting for some day to roll around, he was waiting for a person who has described Himself as "the bright and morning star" (Rev 22:16).

As a true Israelite, the psalmist closes his song with a fervent exhortation. "Let Israel hope in the LORD: for with the LORD there is mercy, and with him is plenteous redemption. And he shall redeem Israel from all his iniquities" (Ps 130:7-8). God has not cast away His people whom He foreknew. "There shall come out of Sion the Deliverer, and shall turn away ungodliness from Jacob" (Ro 11:26). The psalmist had already stated that there is forgiveness with Him (Ps 130:4). To this he now adds mercy, or lovingkindness, and redemption. All of Israel's future blessing is wrapped up in these great words.

"O the depth of the riches both of the wisdom and knowledge of God! how unsearchable are his judgments, and his ways past finding out! For who hath known the mind of the Lord? or who hath been his counsellor? Or who hath first given to him, and it shall be recompensed to him again? For of him, and through him, and to him, are all things: to whom be glory for ever. Amen" (Ro 11:33-36).

> Depth of mercy! can there be
> Mercy still reserved for me?
> Can my God His wrath forbear—
> Me, the chief of sinners, spare?
>
> I have long withstood His grace,
> Long provoked Him to His face,
> Would not hearken to His calls,
> Grieved Him by a thousand falls.
>
> Now incline me to repent;
> Let me now my sins lament;
> Now my foul revolt deplore,
> Weep, believe, and sin no more.
>
> There for me the Saviour stands,
> Holding forth His wounded hands;
> God is love! I know, I feel,
>   Jesus weeps and loves me still.
>
> CHARLES WESLEY

32

PSALM 140
The Day of Battle

WHEN OUR LORD was here on earth, He predicted that history would repeat itself, and that as it was in the days of Noah, so shall it also be in the days of the Son of man (Lk 17:26). According to the biblical record, the days of Noah were days when "the wickedness of man was great in the earth, and that every imagination of the thoughts of his heart was only evil continually. . . . The earth also was corrupt before God, and the earth was filled with violence" (Gen 6:5, 11). Almost every day's newscast could be summed up in these same words. Robbery, rape, and murder make up a large part of the news. Pornography and homosexuality are so freely discussed that even non-Christians are repelled by it all. The late President Eisenhower once said, "We live not in an instant of danger, but in an age of danger." And the apostle Paul wrote, "Evil men and seducers shall wax worse and worse, deceiving, and being deceived" (2 Ti 3:13).

The opening verses of our psalm might have been written yesterday, so accurate is their description of the condition of the world today. The satanic forces back of all this are aptly described in Psalm 140:3: "They have sharpened their tongues like a serpent; adders' poison is under their lips." It is the avowed purpose of these forces to overthrow the "goings" of the child of God (v. 4). His every movement is watched by the enemy. The snare, the cords, the net, and the gins, or, traps (v. 5), present an array of devices intended to ruin every department of a man's life—personal, social, business, and religious. The enemy will employ every means possible to overthrow the child of God. These are the "devices" of Satan by which, if possible, he would "get an advantage of us" (2 Co 2:11).

143

It was such things that led the psalmist to pray, "Thou art my God: hear the voice of my supplications, O LORD. O GOD the Lord, the strength of my salvation, thou hast covered my head in the day of battle" (Ps 140:6-7). The *day* here need not be limited to a day of twenty-four hours. It could include the whole of one's lifetime. It is a time when one needs to be armed, not with physical armor, but with "the whole armour of God" in order that he "may be able to stand against the wiles [or, methods] of the devil" (Eph 6:11). "For the weapons of our warfare are not carnal, but mighty through God to the pulling down of strong holds; Casting down imaginations, and every high thing that exalteth itself against the knowledge of God, and bringing into captivity every thought to the obedience of Christ" (2 Co 10:4-5).

It is our responsibility to take this armor unto ourselves. In the days of Saul and Jonathan, we read, "There was no smith found throughout all the land of Israel: for the Philistines said, Lest the Hebrews make them swords or spears. . . . So it came to pass in the day of battle, that there was neither sword nor spear found in the hand of any of the people that were with Saul and Jonathan: but with Saul and with Jonathan his son was there found" (1 Sa 13:19, 22).

The Philistines of that day have their modern counterparts in the professing church of today who withhold from those under their care the ministry which would equip them to overcome the enemy of souls. Just why Saul and Jonathan did not urge their brethren to equip themselves in like manner is hard to understand. Could it be that the rank and file were content to let Saul and Jonathan fight their battles for them?

But armor, by itself, is not enough. "The children of Ephraim, being armed, and carrying bows, turned back in the day of battle" (Ps 78:9). They turned back because "they kept not the covenant of God, and refused to walk in his law; And forgat his works, and his wonders that he had shewed them" (Ps 78:10-11). A soldier may be well armed, but if he is undisciplined and does not obey orders, he cannot expect victory. If we expect to win in this war, even our thoughts must be brought into captivity "to the obedience of Christ."

Perhaps that is why the head is mentioned in a special way in this psalm (Ps 140:7). We are so prone to try to match our "brains" against the wisdom of God. Intellectualism has been the ruin of more than one servant of God. It is for this reason that we are warned lest any man spoil us "through philosophy and vain deceit" (Col 2:8). Our best protection is "the helmet of salvation, and the sword of the Spirit, which is the word of God" (Eph 6:17). With such protection on our heads and with such a weapon in our hands, we will be able to overcome the tongues which have been sharpened "like a serpent," and the lips which have been poisoned with "adders' poison."

"The fiery darts of the wicked" (Eph 6:16) are inflamed with implacable hatred. Our Lord said, "If the world hate you, ye know that it hated me before it hated you. If ye were of the world, the world would love his own: but because ye are not of the world, but I have chosen you out of the world, therefore the world hateth you" (Jn 15:18-19). It is not because of some offence we may have given to the world, or some injury inflicted upon it; it is simply because we belong to Him, "that the word might be fulfilled that is written in their law, They hated me without a cause" (Jn 15:25).

This then, is what we are to expect in a world like this. "For even hereunto were ye called: because Christ also suffered for us, leaving us an example, that ye should follow his steps. . . . Who, when he was reviled, reviled not again; when he suffered, he threatened not; but committed himself to him that judgeth righteously" (1 Pe 2:21, 23).

Psalm 140:12-13 goes on to say, "I know that the LORD will maintain the cause of the afflicted, and the right of the poor. Surely the righteous shall give thanks unto thy name: the upright shall dwell in thy presence." And with this, the words of the New Testament agree, "Seeing it is a righteous thing with God to recompense tribulation to them that trouble you; And to you who are troubled rest with us, when the Lord Jesus shall be revealed from heaven with his mighty angels . . . when he shall come to be glorified in his saints, and to be admired in all them that believe" (2 Th 1:6-7, 10).

"Be patient therefore, brethren, unto the coming of the Lord. . . . Stablish your hearts: for the coming of the Lord draweth nigh" (Ja 5:7-8).

> Stand up, stand up for Jesus,
> Ye soldiers of the cross,
> Lift high His royal banner,

It must not suffer loss;
From vict'ry unto vict'ry,
His army shall He lead,
Till every foe is vanquished
And Christ is Lord indeed.

Stand up, stand up for Jesus,
Stand in His strength alone;
The arm of flesh will fail you—
Ye dare not trust your own;
Put on the gospel armor,
Each piece put on with prayer;
Where duty calls, or danger,
Be never wanting there.

Stand up, stand up for Jesus,
The strife will not be long;
This day the noise of battle,
The next, the victor's song;
To him that overcometh,
A crown of life shall be;
He with the King of glory
Shall reign eternally.

GEORGE DUFFIELD

33

PSALM 142

Overwhelmed

As MOST OF US have discovered, the child of God is not exempt from the trials and tribulations which are the common lot of all men. In addition to these, he is also exposed to pressures and trials that the world knows nothing about. These things affect him spiritually, emotionally, and physically, as indicated in Psalm 142:3, 4, and 6.

Such experiences are intended to be part of his education, or, instruction, as indicated in the word *Maschil* in the title of this psalm. The word *Maschil* means instruction.

The particular incident which occasioned this psalm took place in a cave. If this was the cave of Adullam (1 Sa 22), David must have had plenty of company because, "There with him about four hundred men." But no mention is made of them in Psalm 142. One can be very lonesome even in a crowd.

But if there was no human ear into which he could pour his troubles, there was one who is always ready to listen to the cry of His desolate child. Even if he had companions in his misery, he did not turn to them. Instead he went directly to the Lord Himself. "I cried unto the LORD with my voice; with my voice unto the LORD did I make my supplication. I poured out my complaint before him; I shewed before him my trouble" (vv. 1-2).

What his complaint and his trouble were is seen in verses 3, 4, 6, and 7. In the way in which he walked some had hidden a snare for him; no man cared for his soul; he was persecuted and imprisoned. In his threefold distress he turned to the only one who could help him, the Lord Himself. In so doing he has set us a good example. When in trouble, we are prone to appeal to some fellow-

147

Christian or to the pastor or minister instead of exercising our God-given right to go directly to the Lord Himself.

Something happened in my boyhood days which may serve as an illustration. Radio, or "wireless," as it was called in those days, was just becoming generally known. Like a lot of other lads, I got interested in this new means of communication and soon had a small set rigged up in my room at home. It was rather crude, to be sure. I had gathered the materials from various sources, including little bits of wire left behind by workmen as they wired new homes for electricity. Bit by bit I assembled all the parts indicated on the little diagram I had purchased to guide me in setting up my little radio receiver. I learned the Morse code so that I might be able to interpret the signals as they came in. Finally the day came when I thought all was complete. To celebrate, I invited the whole family to my room to see and hear this wonderful thing. With a flourish I threw in the switch and adjusted the tuning coil, but alas, there was not a sound to be heard. I was so disappointed that I burst into tears and ran out of the room. My father followed me and very kindly suggested that I go down to the basement where he kept his tools and materials, and bring up a coil of wire he had there.

While I was doing this, he looked over my diagram, and by the time I got back, he had most of the parts disconnected. It looked as though he had wrecked the whole thing. But when he reassembled it, he used one piece of wire where I had used five or six; plus making other improvements. When he had it all back in place, he said to me, "Now try it." Very humbly I put on the earphones, threw in the switch, and lo and behold, the signals came in nice and clear! It was a message from some ship nearing the port of New York. You may be sure I was thrilled. But I was curious to know why it had not worked for me.

Turning to Dad, I said, "Why didn't it work before?"

He simply replied, "I guess you had a loose connection somewhere." That was altogether likely because of the many little bits of wire I had used to make the connections. My father was not slow to make a spiritual application. He reminded me that the best preacher I ever heard, or even the most devout Christian I knew, might prove to be a loose connection between myself and the

Lord. There is nothing like a "hot line" to the throne of grace. That is what the psalmist used.

In presenting his troubles to the Lord, David began at the top. "My spirit was overwhelmed within me" (Ps 142:3). We have different ways of saying this today. It is the kind of a situation that drives some to drink, or to drugs, or even to suicide. Then to discover that someone actually plotted your ruin and secretly laid a snare for you, would make matters even worse. How good then to be able to turn to one who knows exactly what to do about it. "Then thou knewest my path" (v. 3). Even though these words were spoken long before the Lord Jesus came to dwell among us, we can see how well they describe Him who was tried in all points like as we are, and He can be touched with the feeling of our infirmities (Heb 4:15). Yes, He knows our path from personal experience.

To be ignored is another very sore trial for some. "I looked on my right hand, and beheld, but there was no man that would know me: refuge failed me; no man cared for my soul" (Ps 142:4). The soul of man is the seat of his emotions. This part of man's being has been the subject of much study in recent years. But here again nothing is more effective than a direct approach to the Lord Himself. "I cried unto thee, O LORD: I said, Thou art my refuge and my portion in the land of the living" (v. 5). It was when he cried to the Lord that he made the wonderful discovery that the Lord was not only his refuge but his portion as well. He found in the Lord a place of safety and security, and a satisfying portion for his soul also. The Lord had done for him exceeding abundantly above all that he asked or thought (Eph 3:20). And all it cost him was the cry of faith.

In Psalm 142 verse 6, we see the psalmist down again. He says, "I was brought very low." Here it is no longer the snare laid in secret, nor the fact that he was ignored. This was bitter persecution by those who were stronger than he. It would appear that he prayed for death because he said, "Bring my soul out of prison" (v. 7). He wanted to be where the wicked cease from troubling and where the weary are at rest (Job 3:17).

And that marks a change from the minor to the major key: "That I may praise thy name" (Ps 142:7). When that time comes, he finds himself surrounded by many others of like precious faith. "The righteous shall compass me about: for thou shalt deal bountifully with me" (v. 7). What a glorious future!

It is interesting to observe that the psalmist uses three tenses in this psalm. In verse 3, he refers to the past, "Thou knewest my path." In verse 5, he tells the Lord what *He* is to him now. "Thou art my refuge and my portion in the land of the living." In the last verse, he looks on to the future, "Thou shalt deal bountifully with me." In each of these there is a direct reference to the Lord, the one "which is, and which was, and which is to come" (Rev 1:4): "Jesus Christ the same yesterday, and to day, and for ever" (Heb 13:8).

> O God, our help in ages past,
> Our hope for years to come,
> Our shelter from the stormy blast,
> And our eternal home!
>
> Under the shadow of Thy throne
> Still may we dwell secure;
> Sufficient is Thine arm alone,
> And our defense is sure.
>
> Before the hills in order stood,
> Or earth received her frame,
> From everlasting Thou art God,
> To endless years the same.
>
> O God our help in ages past,
> Our hope for years to come,
> Be Thou our guide while life shall last,
> And our eternal home!
>
>   ISAAC WATTS

34

2 SAMUEL 1:17-27

How Are the Mighty Fallen!

To write an ode to victory is one thing; to write an elegy, whose refrain is one of defeat, is quite different. Because of its nature the lamentation which David made over Saul and Jonathan, recorded in 2 Samuel 1:17-27, though not included in the book of the Psalms, may be rightly included in this study. It is actually a Maschil psalm—*Maschil* means instruction, and this passage is full of instruction, as we shall see. The author "bade them teach the children of Judah the use of the bow" (2 Sa 1:18). The bow was the weapon with which the Philistines wounded Saul when "the battle went sore against Saul, and the archers hit him; and he was sore wounded of the archers" (1 Sa 31:3).

The song is concerned with the death of a king and a prince who belonged to the tribe of Benjamin. Their dynasty came to a tragic end on Mount Gilboa. Even though David knew that he was divinely chosen to succeed Saul, he manifests nothing but sorrow at the tidings of his death. It is striking indeed that the crown of "the house of Israel" (2 Sa 1:12) should fall into David's hands as it did.

The earlier part of 2 Samuel 1 gives an account of how an Amalekite, who claimed to have escaped out of the camp of Israel, told David that Saul had asked him to stand on him and kill him, even though his life was yet whole in him. If we accept as authentic the account of Saul's death given in 1 Samuel 31, and I do, then this is fiction. No doubt the Amalekite hoped to gain favor with David, but in that he was mistaken. David would never be indebted to an Amalekite to gain the crown of "the house of Israel." Instead of rewarding the Amalekite, "David took hold on his clothes, and rent them; and likewise all the men that were with him: And

151

they mourned, and wept, and fasted until even, for Saul, and for Jonathan his son, and for the house of Israel; because they were fallen by the sword" (2 Sa 1:11-12).

The first thing that David did after this was to deal with the Amalekite according to his own words. Calling one of his young men, he said, "Go near, and fall upon him. And he smote him that he died. And David said unto him, Thy blood be upon thy head; for thy mouth hath testified against thee, saying, I have slain the LORD's anointed." David did not allow personal feelings to make him overlook what that Amalekite claimed to have done to his king. Neither did he allow personal feelings to keep him from openly acknowledging what was "lovely and pleasant" in the lives of Saul and Jonathan.

David begins his song on a lofty note—"the beauty [or, glory] of Israel." A very similar expression is used to describe our Lord Jesus (Lk 2:32). In ascribing such honor to Saul and Jonathan, David was completely honest. He was not flattering the dead to gain favor with the living. He did not have to do that because he was already a general favorite. His men referred to him later as "the light of Israel," a compliment indeed (2 Sa 21:17).

Saul and Jonathan were slain in the "high places" (2 Sa 1:19). Surely, something more than physical elevation is in view here, even though Mount Gilboa might be described as such. Saul and his son occupied places of highest honor in Israel. Because of that, they would be especially vulnerable (cf. 2 Ch 18:29-34). The application of this to those in "high places" today is simple enough. Had the rank and file been as well armed as Saul and Jonathan (1 Sa 13:22), this story might have had a different ending. Instead of a paean of victory, they now have to lament, "How are the mighty fallen!" (2 Sa 1:19).

The Philistines were not slow in publishing the defeat of Saul and his sons "in the house of their idols, and among the people" (1 Sa 31:9). They even added insult to injury by putting Saul's armor "in the house of Ashtaroth [female deities]: and they fastened his body to the wall of Bethshan" (1 Sa 31:10). But the people of Israel were to have no part in that, even though they had to admit the truth of it. "Tell it not in Gath, publish it not in the streets of Askelon; lest the daughters of the Philistines rejoice, lest the daughters of the uncircumcised triumph" (2 Sa 1:20).

Even the ground which was soaked with the blood of the slain was not to know the blessings of the dew and the rain, in order to yield wave-offerings, because, "There the shield of the mighty is vilely cast away, the shield of Saul, as though he had not been anointed with oil" (v. 21).

Other translations refer the anointing here to the shield of Saul. It was the custom to anoint leather shields with oil. The leather was oiled before battle, either to preserve it or to make it glisten (Is 21:5). The shield of Saul was vilely cast away as if it were worthless. But the shield of faith, freshly anointed with the oil of the Spirit, may serve again to quench all the fiery darts of the wicked one (Eph 6:16). "Cast not away therefore your confidence, which hath great recompense of reward" (Heb 10:35).

Both Saul and Jonathan were skilled in the use of the weapons of war. "From the blood of the slain, from the fat of the mighty, the bow of Jonathan turned not back, and the sword of Saul returned not empty" (2 Sa 1:22; 1 Sa 14:1-14, 47-48). But that was only a memory now. Previous victories do not guarantee future successes. Too often success generates pride. And, "Pride goeth before destruction, and an haughty spirit before a fall" (Pr 16:18).

At this point, the psalmist turns from that which was military to that which was more personal. "Saul and Jonathan were lovely and pleasant in their lives, and in their death they were not divided" (2 Sa 1:23). Jonathan remained loyal to his father, even though his soul "was knit with the soul of David, and Jonathan loved him as his own soul" (1 Sa 18:1).

Even though "they were swifter than eagles" and "stronger than lions" (2 Sa 1:23), Saul and Jonathan went down to defeat on the mountains of Gilboa. Neither speed nor strength availed them there. This was one time when the race was not to the swift, nor the battle to the strong (Ec 9:11). Because of this, the daughters of Israel were called upon to weep over Saul who clothed them in scarlet, with other delights, and put ornaments of gold on their apparel (2 Sa 1:24). No doubt these beautiful things were part of the spoils of war, tokens of past victories and military prowess. This too was only a memory now.

"How are the mighty fallen in the midst of the battle!" (2 Sa 1:25). This is the second time that this refrain occurs in this song, but this time with the added phrase, "in the midst of the battle!" They fell, but they fell fighting! They died facing the foe and not with their backs turned to them. This is further evidence of their courage.

The apostrophe addressed to Jonathan, in 2 Samuel 1:25-26, is very touching. Again there is a reference to the "high places," as if to accentuate his fall. This repeated reference to the high places sounds like a word of warning. Can it be that Jonathan exposed himself unduly? One hesitates to accuse one so noble of anything so foolish. But the personal connection with the high places does give rise to questions, as though his being there was contributory to his fall. But we must not speculate.

Whatever the reason, David was distressed for his "brother Jonathan." The tender and affectionate relationship between these two men has become proverbial. David could never forget the way in which Jonathan defended him before Saul, when "Saul's anger was kindled against Jonathan, and he said unto him, Thou son of the perverse rebellious woman, do not I know that thou hast chosen the son of Jesse to thine own confusion?" Saul even cast a javelin at his son to smite him, so that "Jonathan arose from the table in fierce anger, and did eat no meat the second day of the month: for he was grieved for David, because his father had done him shame" (1 Sa 20:30-34).

David does not speak of his love for Jonathan but only of Jonathan's love for him. "Thy love to me was wonderful, passing the love of women" (2 Sa 1:26). It was a love not based on physical attraction. The Greek translation of the Old Testament here employs the strongest word for love in that language. It is the same word which John used when he said, "Beloved, if God so loved us, we ought also to love one another" (1 Jn 4:11).

The lament closes as it began, with a third reference to the fall of the mighty. "How are the mighty fallen, and the weapons of war perished!" (2 Sa 1:27). But the added phrase here is very striking. It suggests that the mighty who fell were utterly defenseless. It is a sad note on which to conclude. This is truly a psalm in a minor key. But how good to know, "The weapons of our warfare are not carnal, but mighty through God to the pulling down of strong holds" (2 Co 10:4).

Perhaps the saddest thing about this psalm is that there is no reference in it to the life after this. But even that may have a voice for us who are often called upon to speak at the funerals of those who have "fallen asleep." Let us not be content to eulogize the dead, for, "If in this life only we have hope in Christ, we are of all men most miserable" (1 Co 15:19), God grant that all of us may be able to say with Paul, "I have fought a good fight, I have finished my course, I have kept the faith: Henceforth there is laid up for me a crown of righteousness, which the Lord, the righteous judge, shall give me at that day: and not to me only, but unto all them also that love his appearing" (2 Ti 4:7-8).

35

2 SAMUEL 23:1-7

The Last Words of David

THE LAST WORDS of great men are very revealing. The Bible contains the last words of several of them. The last words of Jacob, recorded in Genesis 49, have to do with his twelve sons, their past and future: "Every one according to his blessing he blessed them." He concluded his valediction with minute instructions as to his burial "in the cave that is in the field of Ephron the Hittite."

The last words of Moses, recorded in Deuteronomy 33, also have to do with the tribes of Israel, principally with regard to their future. Unlike Jacob, Moses made no reference to his death or burial. The Lord "buried him in a valley in the land of Moab, over against Beth-peor: but no man knoweth of his sepulchre unto this day" (Deu 34:6).

Joshua's last words were more reminiscent and hortatory than those of Jacob and Moses. He did not single out the tribes by name but addressed the nation as a whole. He was particularly concerned with "the strange gods" that were among them (Jos 24:23), and got them to promise that they would serve the LORD their God, and obey His voice (Jos 23:24). This they did "all the days of Joshua, and all the days of the elders that overlived Joshua, and which had known all the works of the LORD, that he had done for Israel" (Jos 23:31).

Compared with the foregoing examples, the last words of David (2 Sa 23:1-7) are rather brief, with only a passing reference to his house. His main subject is "he that ruleth over men," To begin with, he identifies himself very simply as "David the son of Jesse" (v. 1). He was not ashamed of his humble ancestry as the son of "Jesse the Beth-lehemite" (1 Sa 17:58), even though he was the hero of the hour, having just won a signal victory over Goliath the Philistine. He was the youngest of eight sons (1 Sa 16:11). What mattered more than his place in that large family was the fact that he was the Lord's choice to be the leader of His people, so that he could rightly speak of himself as "the man who was raised up on high" (2 Sa 23:1). When "the LORD had given him rest round about from all his enemies" and he wanted to build the LORD a house, the LORD sent Nathan the prophet to him, saying, "Thus saith the LORD of hosts, I took thee from the sheepcote, from following the sheep, to be ruler over my people, over Israel: And I was with thee whithersoever thou wentest, and have cut off all thine enemies out of thy sight, and have made thee a great name, like unto the name of the great men that are in the earth" (2 Sa 7:1, 8-9).

He was also "the anointed of the God of Jacob" (2 Sa 23:1). In using this name for God, David emphasized God's grace in choosing him for this great honor. David was actually anointed three times. The first time was "in the midst of his brethren: and the Spirit of the LORD came upon David from that day forward" (1 Sa 16:13). On that occasion he was anointed unto the Lord Himself (1 Sa 16:3). From Psalm 23:5 we gather that this was a continuous and abiding anointing.

The second anointing took place in Hebron where the men of Judah anointed him king over that tribe (2 Sa 2:4, 7). Later he was anointed again to be king over all of Israel (2 Sa 5:3, 17). It was when the Philistines heard about this that they sought him, evidently to kill him (1 Co 14:8).

The anointing mentioned in our present portion had to do with his ministry as "the sweet psalmist of Israel" (2 Sa 23:1). In direct connection with that, he says that the Spirit of the Lord spake by him, and that His word was in his tongue. This seems to identify this anointing with that which took place "in the midst of his brethren," before he was anointed to be king over either Judah or Israel.

That he was indeed the "sweet psalmist of Israel" is substantiated by the fact that at least half of the psalms contained in the book of Psalms are ascribed to him. No doubt some of the psalms without titles are his work also. In all of this ministry he was but the mouthpiece of the Spirit of the LORD. It was His word that was on his tongue.

Many of the psalms, as we have seen, have to do with the experiences of God's people. These "last words" are concerned primarily with Him who is the central subject of all Holy Scripture. It should be noted that in that connection the psalmist speaks of God as the God of Israel, and the Rock of Israel. That is in keeping with the majestic subject now before him; namely, that he that rules over men must be a just ruler, ruling in the fear of God. He must be a beneficent despot, but not a tyrant. (Our Lord is called a despot in such passages as Lk 2:29 and Ac 4:24 in the Greek.)

This has in view the millennial reign of our Lord when the world will know for the first time in its history what a reign of absolute righteousness, tempered with mercy, is like. It will be the dawn of a new day when the righteous Ruler will appear "like the light of the morning," or, as He describes Himself, as "the root and the offspring of David, and the bright and morning star" (Rev 22:16). Then to those that fear His name "shall the Sun of righteousness arise with healing in his wings" (Mal 4:2), the dawn of a day without clouds. And the tender grass springing out of the earth by clear shining after rain will symbolize the resurrection of a generation which had become like the grass that withers, and the flower that fades (Is 40:7). The time of the singing of birds will have come (Song 2:12).

Then the righteous Ruler "shall come down like rain upon the mown grass: as showers that water the earth. In his days shall the righteous flourish; and abundance of peace so long as the moon endureth. He shall have dominion also from sea to sea, and from the river unto the ends of the earth" (Ps 72:6-8).

In contrast to all of this, the psalmist has to confess that his house is not so with God. His own failures, as well as those of his successors, sadly confirm that truth of that statement. The seeds he sowed multiplied from generation to generation so that God had to set his house aside altogether. But God did not forget His covenant which was not temporary but everlasting, "ordered in all things and sure" (2 Sa 23:5). He will yet give to His people "the sure mercies of David" (Ac 13:34). For this, says the psalmist, "is all my salvation, and all my desire" even though, for the time being, "he make it not to grow" (2 Sa 23:5). His faith in a covenant-keeping God was firm.

In still darker contrast he speaks of the sons of Belial, the children of the wicked one, who are likened to thorns that cannot be taken with hands (v. 6). This fruitless condition is not due to any lack on God's part. "For the earth which drinketh in the rain that cometh oft upon it, and bringeth forth herbs meet for them by whom it is dressed, receiveth blessing from God: But that which beareth thorns and briers is rejected, and is nigh unto cursing; whose end is to be burned" (Heb 6:7-8).

And so the last song of David ends on a sad note. The last chapter in the Bible would end in the same way, were it not for "that blessed hope," the coming again of the Lord Jesus. The dominant note in this psalm is in that key. These are days when many are praying for the coming of the righteous Ruler over men of whom the Rock of Israel speaks here. "He is the Rock, his work is perfect: for all his ways are judgment: a God of truth and without iniquity, just and right is he" (Deu 32:4).

Never, so it seems, have we had greater reason to believe that His coming is near, even at the doors. "When these things begin to come to pass, then look up, and lift up your heads; for your redemption draweth nigh" (Lk 21:28).

"He which testifieth these things saith, Surely I come quickly. Amen. Even so, come, Lord Jesus. The grace of our Lord Jesus Christ be with you all. Amen" (Rev 22:20-21).